"A book calling for si _____ re _____ y of spiritual
equilibrium is now mo _____ re needed _____ s. A failing world
order, a failing econom _____ , and a continuing clash of arms, all distract
from the one thing needful. May those who read this attentively
find that one needful thing who is Christ and who tells us in His
Scripture, 'Be still and know that I am God.'"

-Alexander Golitzin, Archbishop of Dallas, the South, and the
Bulgarian Diocese – Orthodox Church in America

"This book by Sr. Jeanne Marie Graham, OCD, is truly a gift.
Drawing from her own personal experience, from several spiritual
masters, and from what science teaches us about mind and body, she
offers sage and practical advice on how we can grow in our spiritual
life. Reading this book will assist readers to mature in faith, hope,
and love and to realize more fully their fundamental identity and
vocation as created in the imago Dei."

-Thomas D. Stegman, S.J., Dean and Professor of New Testament,
Boston College School of Theology & Ministry

"A deeply personal interweaving of the psychological and spiritual,
and the journey towards self and otherness in ways that are both
dynamic and seemingly divine. Sr. Jeanne Marie does a masterful
job of blending these perspectives, often through her own intimate
experiences, as a means of painting a mosaic of the human condition
in ways that are both profound and transcendent. For those exploring
faith and a deeper transformation of themselves, this book is sure to
be moving."

-Samuel Justin Sinclair, Ph.D., Clinical Psychologist in Private
Practice

SOUL STIRRINGS

Awakening to the Soul within You

Jeanne Marie Graham

ARCHWAY
PUBLISHING

Archway Publishing books may be ordered through booksellers or by contacting:

Archway Publishing
1663 Liberty Drive
Bloomington, IN 47403
www.archwaypublishing.com
844-669-3957

ISBN: 978-1-6657-2164-6 (sc)
ISBN: 978-1-6657-2166-0 (hc)
ISBN: 978-1-6657-2165-3 (e)

Library of Congress Control Number: 2022906624

Print information available on the last page.

Archway Publishing rev. date: 08/30/2022

CONTENTS

Part III—The Life of Living Love

INTRODUCTION

When I was young, lilac breezes and pastel-blooming trees signaled my favorite time of year. March's dreariness and dark April showers gave way to the unclouded newness of May. Birds sang, baby squirrels played, and mourning doves cooed. The sun was bright, and the trees were a vivid yellow-green against deep blue skies. The earth was born again. A "new creation" was appearing. You could see it, smell it, and touch it. The book of Genesis says that God walked in the "breezy" time of day with Adam and Eve in paradise. Mystics mention four o'clock in the afternoon as the breezy time. I think God loved to walk at four o'clock in May. With lilac breezes. Smiling within His "new creation."

Before my only sister, Jacquie, was born, I had an imaginary friend named Dado. Wherever I was, Dado was with me. Before I could talk, my mother said that I prattled to Dado. His name was one of the first words I spoke. If I received candy or a cookie, I asked for one for Dado. Then I ate it myself. My mother was a little concerned and spoke to our family doctor, who said an imaginary friend was common for the oldest child, so she stopped worrying. I played with Dado all day long. I was never afraid; I was never lonely. I was never alone because Dado was with me. Those feelings have been with me my whole life: hidden, secure, constant.

When I was twenty-eight, that secret friendship and the beginning of a new creation, all played roles in a long journey leading me from a career as a corporate marketing executive to a very *surprising* vocation—that of a cloistered, contemplative, Carmelite nun.

Our lives are a mystery, but there are clues. Our souls recognize these clues. They stir us on. Our lives on this earth are the story of our souls' adventure. It is a love story. It began before time and is still going on. And it will go on. Forever.

Come and See

Growing up in South Boston, my family lived one block from the beach. The smell of the ocean, low or high tide, is one of the things I love most. Behind us lived the Flynn Family. Ray was the former mayor of Boston and was later US ambassador to the Vatican. I babysat the two oldest boys, little Ray and Eddie. In the summer, with the windows open and the ocean breezes flowing, I would hear Kathy Flynn yelling out her window to her younger son, who was getting into something, telling him, "Eddie, God's watching you!" I would smile, wondering what Eddie was up to, but the phrase stuck. *God's watching you.* It is true. God is watching us—not to punish, but with a loving and tender watchfulness. St. Paul says, "In Him, we live, move, and have our being" (Acts: 17:28).

The spiritual life is a recognition of God's presence in our lives. We have personal lives, work lives, and single, married, or family lives. Our spiritual lives are another life. It is life for our souls and the foundation of the grace sustaining the rest of our lives. This life needs to be valued, nurtured, and strengthened. Otherwise, we are living an existence with our souls, bodies, and minds sensing a lack. Something is missing. There is a longing unfulfilled. We can mask it with things, activities, people, and work, but the longing for God is built into us. It is hardwired into our souls. We need God.

Developing a spiritual life is a journey. It is begun one step at a time. It is more than acquiring knowledge or learning to pray, reading about wonderful people and incredible saints, or becoming more involved with your church, temple, mosque, or favorite charity—though you may do all that. It is a relationship.

It is a new *way of life* that changes you, transforms you. You are never the same. I know. I lived it and will share my story.

Many people desire a deeper connection to their souls. This book will share paths to making this deeper connection. It draws on what I have experienced as well as presents the wisdom of great teachers and masters of the spiritual life from which I have learned. This book is structured in parts as a journey.

Jesus, in the Gospel of John, called himself, "the Way, the Truth, and the Life" (John 14:16). There are three parts to this book: "The Way of Living Faith," "The Truth of Living Hope," and "The Life of Living Love." Within each milestone of the journey is a life-changing phase that builds upon the former, as follows: the seeker, the beginner, the believer, the learner, the server, and the leader.

Journeying ahead of his future apostles, Andrew and John, Jesus looked back at them kindly and asked, "What are you looking for?" (John 1:38). They responded, "Where are you staying?" (John 1:38). These next words of Jesus, "Come and you will see" (John 1:39) *stirred* them to leave everything and begin to follow Him. It was four o'clock in the afternoon. The breezy time.

So, I ask you, what are you looking for at this present time in your life? Gently close your eyes, take a deep breath, and ask this of yourself. I invite *you* to enter into *your love story. Your soul's adventure.* My prayers are with you.

PART I

The Way of Living Faith

ONE
The Seeker

A MATTER OF TIME

God has made everything appropriate
to its time, but has put the timeless
into their hearts so they cannot find out, from
beginning to end, the work which God has done.
—Ecclesiastes 3:11

As children, many of us lived our first years in the "timeless land of wonder." We were seekers and explorers from the time we first opened our eyes and took our first steps. Everything was a new experience, every day a new adventure. Some of my favorite childhood memories took place at my grandparents' home. They lived in the country, by a reservoir, about an hour south from Boston. Life slowed down considerably there. *Literally.*

Traveling to their house after the highway, right before entering Norton, where they lived, was a huge, sharp slope in the road. We called it "Nana's bump." Most cars would slowly go over it. As we approached, my sister and I would yell, "Here comes Nana's bump!" and my dad would accelerate, speeding over it as the car soared in the air and our stomachs lifted like on a roller-coaster ride. Next to their house, my family had a small cottage where we spent the summer. However, my grandparents' home had a year-round "vacation" feel to it. Many of those living around them were retired. Everyone took life easy. Their house was in a grove, which was like a huge cul-de-sac with many roads, but only two exits and entrances. The only cars you would see were those of the people living there. The roads were very narrow, and in the summer, we would stop our bikes for the slowing cars to pass us by. The drivers and passengers would wave, say hello, and tell us to be careful. Everyone knew each other, and smiles were everywhere. Summer evenings after dinner, neighbors would walk the grove and then end up at the beach to watch the sun go down. I remember those sunsets, mirrored on the lake, as absolutely spectacular.

Maybe it was because I was so happy there that the days seemed to go on forever. There was so much beauty and wonder to see and explore, including lagoons, water dams, and pathways to blueberry bushes. My sister and I were friends with a few other kids who lived in the grove or, like us, had summer homes there. We spent time together collecting grasshoppers, turtles, and frogs. We climbed trees, listened to top-forty hits, went swimming, rode our bikes, played Yahtzee, and sat in tree houses for hours. Everything was fresh and green. Everything was captivating—even watching ants build anthills. From morning to sundown every day, life was unhurried, fun, beautiful, and peaceful. It was like heaven—an earthly paradise.

Looking back, it seems we were all living soulfully, and time in that place was eternal. It is hard to re-create those childhood summer days. The closest I can now come to those feelings of timeless peace is when I am on my yearly retreat. A retreat is like a vacation, only you go on this vacation seeking God. It is a time of silence, solitude, prayer, and renewal. A time to get in touch with your soul. Carmelites spend retreats alone in a separate section of their monasteries, but most retreat centers are located in spiritual settings of natural beauty in the woods or by mountains, oceans, or lakes. During a retreat, time slows down. From the beginning of the weekend, or a one- or two-week retreat, you are encouraged to put your watch, iPad, and cell phone away and *just be.*

The incredible beauty of nature and this letting go of time sets the tone for an experience of God. To seek Him, our souls need ease, stillness, and freedom. Our bodies—specifically, our eyes, ears, and minds—need beauty, silence, desire, and rest. Most retreatants begin their first nights of retreat by sleeping very deeply, not realizing how tired and emotionally drained they are until they are still before God and away from it all.

We need that time alone to find ourselves again—our true, childlike selves, where our souls dwell. When we find our true selves, we can then easily find God. Spiritual seeking is a going out of ourselves into otherness, to later return to ourselves again, renewed and refreshed. This requires time—time we need to invest not in the stock market or the gym, but in our spiritual well-being.

The Greeks had two expressions for time: *kairos* and *chronos.* Chronos time is the ticking clock. In ancient Greek mythology, Cronus was the god of time. Time was described as a destructive, all-crushing power. Chronos time is a force to be reckoned with. We can be slaves to it. We can feel we never have enough. We are in a constant state of doing, always catching up, planning, and looking forward to the future—a future that may never come.

Kairos time is insightful, contemplative, and eternal. In Greek mythology, Kairos, the youngest child of Zeus, was the god of opportunity. Kairos times are God's moments of grace. They are glimpses of eternity where God is present, gazing at us and loving us. In kairos time, we are present to ourselves and to others. We are not dwelling or living in the past or future; we are mindfully experiencing life as it comes to us in God.

Both chronos and kairos give us a sense of the *now*, but experiencing that present moment in time is completely different for each. Time was created for us as a gift. We are each given a measure of time, and we are to use it wisely. God is beyond time. God is eternal and ever present—always was, always will be. Forever. God's presence is all around us. It is visible and invisible. All beauty is God. Truth is God. Peace is God. Love is God. Wisdom is God. To desire and seek God is wisdom. Our souls (true selves) recognize and thirst in this desire for God. For our souls *are* wisdom, beauty, truth, love, and peace. They live in kairos time.

Our lives and bodies tend to be lost in chronos time. Our lives are driven relentlessly to attain wants and desires that we later find do not fulfill or satisfy us. To change, we need to sharpen our spiritual sight. We need to unlock the door to our souls, regain the ability to recognize the unseen, and become aware of what truly *is*. It is an *opening* to a new dimension of *what is*. Once the door is opened, there is no going back. Existence takes on new meaning. All is different because the truth of our eternal souls has been experienced.

TWO
The Seeker

IN THE BEGINNING

Let us ask ourselves today: are we
open to "God's Surprises"?
—Pope Francis, *The Church of Mercy*

Many people ask me if I always wanted to be a nun and I *always* say no. I was taught by sisters in elementary and high school and appreciated their faith and dedication but never thought of following them into religious life. So my vocation came as a complete surprise to me as well as to my family and my friends. Here is the beginning of the story.

In the second grade, I made my First Communion and received as a gift a book on St. Thérèse, a Carmelite nun who lived in France in the 1800s. I loved it. A year later, we were asked to dress up as our favorite saints on All Saints' Day, and I chose her. Each of us was to give a talk on our saint, so I reread the book. My mother did a great job dying sheets for my religious Carmelite habit and preparing a crucifix adorned with roses. My teacher, Sister Thomas Aquinas, asked me to stay after school that day. She presented me with a ruby glass cross necklace, smiled, and said I did a good job presenting St. Thérèse to the class. I think a seed was planted for a future vocation, unrealized to me at that time.

I later attended Fontbonne Academy, an all-girl college prep school. The sisters of St. Joseph encouraged us to set our dreams high. My dream was a business career, marriage, family, and a beautiful house by the ocean. I wanted three children: boy, girl, boy, in that order. I even had names for consideration: Michael, Lianne, and Christopher. I loved the name Michael.

Two years after graduating from college with a bachelor's degree in economics, I was hired by Polaroid Corporation to manage a retail marketing test site at Quincy Market, a historic tourist center in Boston. A few years later, I went into sales, and that was when I met Michael. At the time, I was living with my sister on Jerusalem Road in Cohasset, Massachusetts. Looking back, it all started, ironically, on Jerusalem Road. We rented a carriage house across the street from the ocean, and it was beautiful. The daily commute was horrendous, but the place was lovely. At twenty-eight I was seriously dating a corporate vice president, whom I had met on a plane, and was on my way to my dream. Or so I thought.

Michael was a Polaroid sales manager from Dallas who was training me in consumer sales. We began in New York City, where he introduced me to the most difficult camera dealers in the US. He was the smoothest salesperson I had ever worked with. During the trip, we found ourselves sitting at a stoplight when an ambulance went by. He had been talking nonstop, and I briefly shut my eyes. It prompted him to ask me if I was okay, and I nodded. He then asked what I was doing. I said I was praying a Hail Mary for the person in the ambulance. He continued to ask why, and I said it was because that was something my mom had taught me to do since I was a child. It had become a habit.

What followed was a two-day discussion on religion. He stated that he was a Baptist and very involved in his church. However, he had difficulty understanding why anyone would pray to Our Lady. I, in turn, as a Catholic, explained our relationship with the Blessed Mother. I prayed the Hail Mary out loud to him and explained it as a form of intercessory prayer. He asked me if I owned a Bible, and I replied that I did not, but we had a family Bible listing all the births and deaths of our relatives. He was dumbfounded as to why I didn't own one. "Don't you read the Bible?" he asked.

I said, "No. I go to Sunday Mass where we have Scripture readings from the Bible with a homily."

Later that year, Michael went to Jerusalem on a pilgrimage and from Dallas sent me a beautiful Bible. It was covered in olive wood from the Holy Land. I still have it and pray with it. I thanked him and put it on a nightstand, never opening it. About a month later, he called me to see how I was doing and then asked if I was reading my Bible. He was on a mission. I said I hadn't but promised him I would that night.

My bedroom had a veranda that looked out to the ocean. Over my bed was a skylight to look at the stars. I remember, before I went to sleep for the night, closing my eyes, opening the Bible, and randomly looking at a page. It was Proverbs 1:7, which says, "The fear of the Lord is the beginning of wisdom, and knowledge of the Lord is understanding." I closed the Bible, shut off the light, and looked up and out at the stars, thinking and repeating the proverb over and over. I then started to read and repeat a proverb every night.

I believe my new spiritual life began as I read and repeated those Proverbs to myself. I had always gone to Mass from childhood, but by my twenties had stopped praying vocal prayers. I remember meditating only once in a Zen class in high school. In that first Proverb passage alone are four of the seven gifts of the Holy Spirit: awe of the Lord, wisdom, knowledge, and understanding. Right from the start, the Holy Spirit was awakening me to my soul.

Angelic Help in Seeking God

The whole air about us is filled with angels.
—St. John Chrysostom

Throughout the history of the world, the Holy Spirit has opened believers' eyes to the reality of God's presence within and around them through the help of powerful and mysterious angels. We live our lives with angels surrounding us. Invisibly. Angels are purely spiritual creatures that have intelligence and will. They are servants and messengers of God and always behold the face of the Father in heaven. They have been present since creation and very instrumental in the history of salvation. Over the last ten years, varying polls reveal that over 80 percent of Americans believe in angels, and many report having experienced their own guardian angels. More than half say they believe that these supernatural agents shape the detail of their lives.

Lorna Byrne is a woman who sees angels. From earliest childhood, she has communicated with the angels who have surrounded her. She has written many number-one bestselling books on angels and has traveled around the world as a peace ambassador. Lorna is currently known as one of the one hundred most spiritually influential living people in the world today. Born in the 1950s in Ireland, like many at that time and in that country, she grew up in a poor family. Labelled mentally handicapped as a child because of her dyslexia, she never finished her primary school education. In the 1970s, Lorna met her husband, Joe Byrne, whom she was told by an angel that she would marry. Joe suffered from seriously ill health and was unable to work much of the time, so the couple and their children lived in poverty. Joe died, leaving Lorna with four children, the youngest only four years old. From a very early age, angels told Lorna that she would write a book about them. She laughed, telling them it was unlikely because she had dyslexia and could hardly read or write. However, in 2003, Lorna started to work on her first book, and in May 2008, *Angels in My Hair,* her memoir, was published in the UK and Ireland. That book and these others, *A Message of Hope from the Angels* and *Love from Heaven* reached number one on the UK Sunday Times Book Chart, as well as becoming *New York Times* best sellers. They have been translated into thirty languages and published in over fifty countries.

In her book *Stairways to Heaven*, she tells the story of how she met a Jewish mother and daughter when she was doing a book signing in Philadelphia in the United States:

> As I was saying goodbye to a woman, an angel tapped me on the shoulder, and pointed down the line saying; "There is a mother and child there who are very nervous. I am the mother's guardian angel. My name is Rosalet." When it was their turn, they walked toward me looking very nervous. The mother sat down on the chair beside me and said, "We are probably not meant to be here. We were unsure whether we would be allowed to come into the shop because this is a Catholic shop and we are Jewish." Up to that moment I hadn't even noticed that it was a Catholic shop and I was shocked that someone of any religion would think that they weren't welcome. The mother added, "Lorna, maybe God hasn't given us Jewish people a guardian angel?" She was still talking in a very hushed voice. I reached out to them both and took their hands, saying urgently, "Don't you know that every single human being has a guardian angel? This is a gift

from God. It doesn't matter what religion you are
or even if you have no beliefs at all. You both have
guardian angels. I can see them both behind you as
clearly as I can see you."

Lorna said that when the mother and daughter left, they
were so happy to know angels were with them. Lorna felt moved
and was surprised they hadn't known about their guardian
angels. She then goes on to declare that all of us individually
have our own angels. She adds, "We are never alone. Our
guardian angel is always with us and is the gatekeeper of our
soul."

Our guardian angels love us unconditionally. Throughout
eternity, we are the only souls they will be entrusted to guide.
They have been with us since our conceptions and will guide
us after our deaths. They have been given to us by God to
protect, help, and love us. Guardian angels, with the Holy Spirit,
work through your soul, influencing your conscience and your
feelings. After sinning or hurting someone, you will feel guilty
or uneasy; that constant disquiet may be prompted by your
guardian angel. Promptings, or the inspiration to begin or
create something, call someone, help a stranger, or even smile,
may be some of the ways you are intuitively directed by your
guardian angel to touch other lives.

On the day of 9/11 in NYC, there were many stories of
people prevented from going to work that morning because it
was not their time to "go home." Those delays or changes in
plans were most likely orchestrated by their guardian angels
according to the will of God. Some believed they were helped
and saved directly by divine intervention. Ron DiFrancesco
was one of only two survivors from the eighty-fourth floor of
Tower Two. He heard a mysterious voice urge him to escape by
means of a stairwell. After he descended, a firefighter held out

a hand to help him. There were burns over the majority of his body. His contact lenses had melted onto his eyes. It took years for him to recover, but he had survived. The thirteenth floor of Tower One collapsed on Genelle Guzman-McMillan, and she believes an angel held her hand for twenty-seven hours until she was pulled from the debris.

When I am aware of my guardian angel, I hear a slight hum in my right ear that I discovered means I am to delay or stop an action. Other times, I feel a light touch on the top of my head, usually when I am anxious or upset. There are times when mechanically something will not work—for no reason. Or there is a delay in another's action while I am waiting. Later, I find out there was a reason for these delays, and it was providential. Occasionally, an orb will appear in photographs above and behind me. Sometimes a feather shows up out of nowhere. These are a few ways I may feel or see the presence of my guardian angel.

Guardian angels will help us to seek God. They will inspire us on the ways to search and encourage us when we are fearful or disillusioned. They pray with us, and most importantly, they *assist us to recognize God's will and action in our lives*. From the times we were in our mother's wombs, they have been with us. They know us and love us. We are never alone. So, learning to perceive them, thanking them for their guidance, and trusting our lives' journeys to them is an excellent way to begin your spiritual lives.

God's Unconditional Love

I call you by name; you are mine.
—Isaiah 43:1

God calls each one of us by name. He has set angels to watch over and guard us. God knows and loves us personally, tenderly, and unconditionally. This love of God the Father is hard to understand if you never received this love as a child. Family life is where love is taught and experienced. As culture changes from generation from generation, so does family life.

According to a 2015 Pew Research study on family life in the US, by 1980, 61 percent of children were living in a family with two married parents in their first marriages. Today, less than half (46 percent) live with both their parents. Twenty-six percent of children younger than age eighteen are now living with a single parent.

Another study found that over a three-year period, about three in ten (31 percent) children younger than six had experienced a major change in their family or household structures. These changes are in the form of parental divorce, separation, marriage, cohabitation, or death. Demonstrative love is also different culturally. Tangible love sentiments, such as hand-holding, hugs, and kisses vary from family to family, even within the same nationality. We tend to hold our families' ways of life as a norm, but experiencing the family lives of others shows us the differences. At times, there are radical differences in their expressions of love or lack of it.

People suppress love. Fear stops them. Our souls *are* love and suffer when they cannot be expressed. To be secure, children need to feel unconditionally loved. If they themselves never felt it at home, they cannot express it. This can lead to feelings of indifference. They fail to show love and find it hard to receive it from others. The soul starts to become darkened from the lack of the light of love. Feelings of anger and fear result in rebellious behaviors, which are just a cry for help. When these feelings are suppressed, they come out in alternate ways. We choose substitutes to numb our hurt, broken emotions like alcohol and drugs. We get lost in iPads and iPhones.

Our souls are like windows that look out onto our worlds through our bodies. They see more than our physical eyes. They perceive life on a deeper level. They recognize goodness, peace, hope, joy, and love, but they also see sin, anger, injustice, pain, fear, and death. I was four when JFK died. Seeing the funeral on TV was one of my earliest experiences. I did not know what was going on. I learned that the president was shot and died. When I asked why, my mother said she did not know. Someone killed him. That was when I learned someone could harm or even kill you.

As we experience sin, anger, pain, and, most of all, fear, we begin to form protective shells that darken the innocence and *freedom* of our souls. Our egos form to protect us. The *I* of self-preservation can later be followed by the *I* of selfishness, pride, and wants. It is gradual, and we do not perceive the subtle changes it makes to our views of life and ways of living. At some point—and it may be as late as middle age—we realize that we are more watchful, less spontaneous, and more guarded. Our wonder and awe have diminished. So has our natural sense of joy.

For some, the time treadmill has been on, and we have been caught in a race toward a goal we set for ourselves: happiness by enculturation. We find out that we have been masterfully, continuously conditioned by education, advertising, consumerism, and social media to "be" something other than who we truly are. In our lives, we sense a disconnect, a kind of dis-ease—a general feeling of discontent that, at its worst, can actually make us sick. Depressed. And we do not know how to fix it.

C. G. Jung, one of the chief founders of modern psychiatry, stated in his classic book, *Modern Man in Search of a Soul*, that most of his patients over thirty-five with deep psychiatric issues had "lost" their sense of soul. "It is safe to say that every one of them fell ill because they had lost that which the living religions of every age have given to their followers, and none of them has been really healed who did not regain their religious outlook."[1]

There is a big difference between the self-love of the soul and the selfishness of the ego. What begins in fear can lead to the extreme, to the sin of self-centeredness.

Achievement, status, money, and how others perceive us may end up more important than family, security, leisure, simple lifestyles, and charitable works—not to mention God. For others, emotional hurts, abuse, or bad choices have created deep wounds that have scarred over the soul's natural light. Forgiveness and healing are needed to restore those disheartened and distressed souls.

Souls seek God. When a soul is enclosed in a body and subjected to thoughts that are unaware, unreceptive or, even worse, hostile to God, it feels chained and jailed. Trapped. Michelangelo helps us to understand this feeling of the soul's entrapment. He once saw a slab of marble and said to himself, "There is an angel trapped in this marble. I am going to liberate him." It took time, motivation, and precise chiseling for Michelangelo to free that angel within.

---

[1] Carl. G. Jung, *Modern Man in Search of a Soul*, 1933, p. 229.

Our souls are greater than angels. We have been made in the *Image of God*. Living, like sculpting, is about chiseling away at the unnecessary and at the external in pursuit of the truth and incredible beauty within. It is about restoring that image and allowing it to live in the freedom of love. It is a shedding of dead weight that we have been carrying for too long that has become meaningless. We need to stop. We need to breathe. We need to be still. That is the work that will restore our peace of mind and joy for living. That is the work that will help us to live nobler, more loving lives, with wisdom and understanding.

That is *the beginning* of the journey back to our child-souls, the path we are seeking. Back home to God.

THREE
The Seeker

SEEKING GOD

In the first place it should be known
that if a person is seeking God,
his Beloved is seeking him much more.
—St. John of the Cross

The desire to seek God comes from our souls. I will repeat that: the desire to seek God comes from our souls. In the midst of our souls is what has been called the "spark of God." The term *spark,* relating to the soul, is very old. It was used by Plotinus, a major philosopher influenced by Plato in AD 270, whose writings have inspired centuries of Islamic, Jewish, and Christian metaphysicians. A metaphysician is a philosopher who studies the fundamental nature of reality and existence itself. *Meta–* means beyond or transcending, so *metaphysical* means that which lies beyond the physical realm, world, or reality. Lorna Byrne, who never read any philosophy or theology in her life but was taught by angels, uses the term "a tiny spark of God" to describe the soul. This spark is a participation in the life of God.

When we die, our souls go on. Our egos are nonexistent. Reports of near-death experiences reveal that the soul, a remaining consciousness, rises above the body, *freed* from the dead weight of the body and, more importantly, the ego.

What is interesting is that for many who have experienced this, when the soul returns to the body, one's sense of the ego has dramatically changed. Fear is gone. Pride is gone. Love has taken over. In some cases, a selfless giving to a mission or a renewed purpose in life is now in place. That after-death experience teaches that who we really are is far beyond our imagining or comprehension.

"Who we really are" has been the object of study in theology, philosophy, mysticism, theosophy, and ontology for thousands of years. At the core of metaphysics is ontology, which is the study of the nature of being, becoming, existence or reality. To the metaphysician, we are immortal souls, sparks of the divine, and it is our souls that give us our consciousness.

Pierre Teilhard de Chardin, a French Jesuit priest, theologian and scientist wrote, "You are not a human being in search of a spiritual experience. You are a spiritual being immersed in a human experience." From the womb, we have a sense of the reality of God's love in our souls. But from childhood, we begin to distort it. Forget it. Lose it like our first parents, Adam and Eve did. Immersed in our minds, engaged in our constant bantering thoughts and the daily construction sites of our egos, we forget who we really are. Years go by. Our lives go by. Many of us have built for ourselves beautiful ivory towers, and the thought of our "beings" as a temple of God does not exist in our minds—only in our *silenced* souls. However, God remains in every moment in our lives, watching and waiting for us to remember. To become aware. Life events, failures, unexplained joys, nature, creativity, and prayer help awaken us to the gentle-yet-determined voices of our consciences, our deep consciousness, our souls who know and love God. Once our consciousness is stirred, it will begin to awaken. That is the beginning of our seeking.

Saints and Mystics

It was not long after my nightly Bible reading that I began what I now call a tentative spiritual seeking. The northeast Polaroid sales office was a few miles away from a great bookstore, the New England Bookmobile Fair. On Fridays during my lunch hour (I traveled the rest of the week), I would browse there, looking for a book for the weekend. It was at this store that I purchased my first two spiritual books, *The Story of a Soul* by St. Thérèse, and *The Spiritual Exercises* by St. Ignatius of Loyola. Both works answered questions, posed others, and certainly stirred my soul. So began the new adventure. The Carmelite, St. John of the Cross, says that God makes Himself known in ways specifically designed for the individual. It is a gentle "giving of Himself in love."

My weekly bookstore shopping became a "treasure hunt" that would result in the next book of new insights, a little more understanding, and a growing secret love. The books had instructions that I would underline or highlight. Unknowingly, I was taking courses in spirituality and studying "the science of the saints." *The Spiritual Exercises* actually stopped me in my tracks, and, while reading, I perceived a slight whisper of a call that I did not understand. However, a distinct conversion was set into action. I felt it in my soul, and there was no denying it.

Here are some of the classic authors whose works I read in the beginning:

Saints—St. Thérèse, St. Ignatius, St. Augustine, St. Teresa of Avila, St. John of the Cross, St. Catherine of Sienna, St. Francis de Sales, St. Thomas Aquinas, St. Francis of Assisi, St. Teresa of Calcutta, St. Thomas a

Kempis, St. Faustina, St. Pio of Pietrelcina, St. Basil of Caesarea, and St. Bonaventure

Spiritual Masters—Thomas Merton, Jean Pierre de Caussade, Author of the Cloud of Unknowing, and Brother Lawrence of the Resurrection

Mystics—Anne Catherine Emmerich, Gabrielle Bossis, and Julian of Norwich

What amazed me was not the extraordinary ways in which these people experienced God—and they were extraordinary—but how varied and personalized their individual experiences and missions were. For example, Mystic Gabrielle Bossis, a French actress and playwright, received private revelations or locutions from Jesus. He spoke to her daily for many years. In her book, *He and I*, based on her journals, she describes the growing, loving relationship between them and relates these words of his, "Each soul is my favorite. I am the Soul of your soul." St. Catherine of Sienna had conversations with God the Father. Her book, *The Dialogues of St. Catherine of Sienna*, is an overview of the spiritual life as expressed by Him. The Father said, "I do not want to violate the rights of your freedom. But as soon as you wish it, I myself transform you into Me and make you one with Me." The Dominican, St. Thomas Aquinas, wrote a huge treatise, *The Summa Theologica*, on the way to know God, and the Carmelite, Brother Lawrence of the Resurrection, wrote a few simple letters.

God can be very direct in His approach when a specific mission is assigned for His kingdom. Similar to St. Paul's conversion, St. Ignatius, founder of the Society of Jesus, the Jesuits, was not "knocked of his horse," but was hit by a cannon ball. Reformer of the Carmelite Order, St. Teresa of Avila's heart was "pierced by an angel's arrow." Her heart is now in a reliquary in Spain. You can actually see the hole. The Franciscan, St. Pio of Pietrelcina, known for most of his life as Padre Pio, was stigmatized with the bleeding wounds of Christ for exactly fifty years ... to the day!

St. Thérèse established "The Little Way," and the Jesuit, Jean Pierre de Caussade, is recognized for his concepts of "The Sacrament of the Present Moment" and "Abandonment to Divine Providence." St. Francis of Assisi, founder of the Franciscans, loved God in creation. St. Teresa of Calcutta, founder of the Missionaries of Charity, loved God in the faces of the poor and dying.

All these people were different but were similar. They were humble. They were courageous. They were obedient. They were wise. They were simple. Yet, each of them had found a way to know, serve and love God. Each listened to their soul. But for each the spiritual journey was begun one step at a time. In faith.

FOUR
The Believer

THE UNKNOWN DEPTH

Faith is to believe what you do not see.
The reward of this faith is to see what you believe.
—St. Augustine

B elief is faith, trust, and confidence in someone or something. It is an acceptance that something is true or exists. A *spiritual* believer generally belongs to a certain religion and follows a set of religious beliefs. The word *religion* comes from a Latin word, *religare*. *Re* means again, and *Ligare* means to connect. In religion, we find the ways and beliefs for reconnecting with God. To get a perspective on religion, allow me to open this chapter with a brief overview.

Despite the loss of faith for many people in our current world, Pew Research Center has gathered some statistics that show us that many are seeking knowledge of their God. World Population Review had these *latest* statistics in 2021:

Worldwide, more than eight in ten people identify with a religious group. Here is the breakdown:

- 2.4 billion Christians
- 1.9 billion Muslims (24 percent)
- 1.16 billion Hindus (15 percent)

- 507 million Buddhists (7 percent)
- 14.6 million Jews (0.2 percent)
- 430 million people (6 percent) practice various folk or traditional religions, including African traditional religions, Chinese folk religions, Native American religions, and Australian aboriginal religions
- 61 million people (1 percent) belong to other religions, including the Baha'i faith, Jainism, Sikhism, Shintoism, Taoism, Tenrikyo, Wicca, and Zoroastrianism

Also reported in the study were the 1.19 billion of the world's population who are not affiliated with any religion.

Every religion has its own strengths, beliefs and practices, history and traditions, rituals and ceremonies, celebrations, and sacrifices. After researching, I found that a few simple principles exist in all faiths. One is the Golden Rule: "Do unto others as you would want them to do unto you." The other is "the transcendence of self," or the seeking of truth, love, and oneness by overcoming the ego/self to attain the final goal of existence. Each religion has its own name for this goal:

- Nirvana—Buddhism
- Moksha—Hinduism
- Bittul—Judaism
- Union with God-Christian

Christianity has a Greek term for transcendence that is called *kenosis*, which is an emptying of ourselves in love for others. By kenosis, we become "one" in Christ and also "one" in God. St. Paul states it in his letter to the Galatians, "It is no longer I that live, but Christ" (Galatians 2:20).

The Journey

The idea of spiritual growth and human existence as a journey is present in all religions. As a child, I remember my fascination with a movie about Buddhist monks. I have tried to look for the name of the movie, but I cannot find it. The cinematography was incredible, but it was the simplicity and beauty of the monastic life that intrigued me. The silence, the gongs, and the meditative mood of the monks moved my soul. I think I was about eleven or twelve years old when I sensed a seed was "sprouting" while I watched that movie.

At a point in the movie, the monks made a mandala, a sand painting of ancient symbols that creates a sacred path. Single grains of sand are dropped, one after another, by a team of four monks, bent over the floor and working for hours—or, in some cases, days. It takes millions of vibrant-colored sand grains to create a mandala. The process is a form of meditation and is considered a sacred experience.

In Tibetan Buddhism, mandalas are created according to religious texts. For example, the Mahavairochana-Sutra says the mandala should be painted in five colors, following a prescribed path from the center to the exterior:

- White, for openness,
- Red, signifying power, the life force,
- Yellow, for humility,
- Blue, for infinity, purity, and life, and
- Black, representing darkness.

Another type of Tibetan mandala has these colors carefully placed according to specific teachings, starting from the center outward:

- White, which represents faith,
- Yellow, showcasing effort,
- Red, representing memory,
- Green, signifying meditation, and
- Blue, indicating wisdom.

Once completed, the monks chant and play instruments in a closing ceremony. Then, using a single finger, a monk will draw lines in the circular artwork, cutting it into four slices, then into eight. Lastly, using a paintbrush, another monk will carve broad strokes into the sand, transforming it into a mass of rainbow color. The monks sweep up the sand and pour it in a nearby river or stream, blessing it and the world around it. The mandala is destroyed because of the fundamental message of Buddhism, "nothing is permanent." The creation of it is an experience, not a work of art.

Buddhists believe everything is always changing, moving to balance and enlightenment. Their spiritual path is called the Noble Eightfold Path with Nirvana as its goal, a transcendent state in which there is neither suffering, desire, nor sense of self.

In 1918, psychiatrist Carl Jung introduced mandalas as a therapeutic tool for exploring the unconscious. The word *psyche* comes from the Greek *psykhe*, which means the soul, spirit, or invisible animating entity which occupies the physical body. In his book *Memories, Dreams and Reflections*, Jung writes, "The Mandala is an archetypal image whose occurrence is attested throughout the ages. It signifies the wholeness of Self. This circular image represents the wholeness of the psychic ground or, to put it in mythic terms … the divinity incarnate in man."

Psychological research reveals that there is a primacy to the unconscious. There is an "unknown" depth within us to explore. It is where our center for faith resides. Artists, scientists, musicians, and poets seek to reveal the unknown, unseen aspects of our souls. In their pursuit of beauty and truth, they express what is within them, lying dormant. They get lost in their expressions. Living in the moment, they lose all sense of time; their souls and spirits take over as they create.

As a means of art therapy, Jung and his patients found that creating mandalas helped to access deeper levels of the psyche. He called it the ultimate tool in exploring the unconscious. Jung's patients were presented with a white sheet of paper with a pencil-drawn circle on it and a box of oil pastels. His directions were simple: "Surprise yourself." Jung discovered an interconnection between spirituality and psychology. He found that we "know" and have made decisions on an unconscious level before we "know" consciously. Jung regularly said that "the psyche will not tolerate self-deception."

We can look at our own lives as vibrant mandalas with millions and millions of actions, steps, thoughts, and decisions that we made daily, using one colorful grain after another. This image of ourselves has layers and layers of informative designs that evoke memories, feelings, dreams, and insights. At the center of all these actions is God, present within our souls. Like a labyrinth, the mandala's center represents the core of reality, the *essence* where a person's spiritual journey actually started and will end.

To get back to the core of reality, the essence of life, the way to truth, we must pray for a new way of seeing, understanding, and reflecting. Our souls need to be fully freed to act. We need to heal and realign. This requires a slow releasing of the ego's hold on our behaviors, which deny and distorts reality, and to grow in surrender to recognize the deeper awareness of the *stifled lives* of our souls.

It is not easy because we inherited an original sin that disturbed that original freedom. Self-created needs and desires taint our souls, affecting our minds' judgements. In paradise, ego disobedience and denial were born. Adam and Eve were aware that a particular event occurred but could not know the implications of that event. The immediate response in the garden of Eden was fear. In the cool of the evening, the breezy time when God walked with love looking for them, they hid themselves.

That first effect of sin created fear of God, where formally there was only love. Originally, our soulful minds and bodies were free, living in a childlike peace and joy, always present, pure, unencumbered, creative, and at one with nature. Aware of God. Present to God. The goal of the spiritual life is a return to this freedom, a return to that former knowing, loving and *being with* God. It is allowing our soul, who recognizes God's action and will to inspire and lead us. God walks with us on our journey of life. He is within us. And we live in Him.

God is, in reality, the *Soul of our souls.*

FIVE
The Believer

THE NATURE OF FAITH

To believe in God is one thing,
to know God is another.
It is impossible to explain.

—St. Siluoan

In his book *The Song of Bernadette,* detailing the apparitions of Our Lady at Lourdes, Franz Werfel wrote, "For those who believe, no explanation is necessary, for those who do not believe, no explanation is possible." Such is the nature of our faith.

What we believe sets the foundation for our lives. Our daily actions flow from our beliefs. They are part of who we are. Belief is the truth we live by. We witness our beliefs by the values and standards we set for ourselves and our children. From our integrity, the consistent need to "walk the talk," our children learn honesty, trust, dependability, and moral behavior. Living a life of integrity means we listen to our souls. Our consciences are informed, and we try to always do the right thing. This makes our lives simple and our actions transparent.

To live this way, within our own sense of truth, requires making right choices based on values and principles on which we have reflected. Living by reflection is an integral step in knowing ourselves and knowing what we stand for. Characteristics such as honesty, keeping promises, remaining true to your word, taking responsibility for your actions, and owning up to mistakes are all related to a person's integrity. The following wonderful, inspirational story is found on the website *Purpose Focus Commitment*. The website has many incredible stories encouraging moral values such as integrity and truth.

> *A successful businessman was growing old and knew it was time to choose a successor to take over the business. He called all the young executives in his company together.*
>
> *"It is time for me to step down and choose the next CEO. I have decided to choose one of you." The young executives were shocked, but the boss continued, "I am going to give each one of you a seed today—one very special seed. I want you to plant the seed, water it, and come back here one year from today with what you have grown from the seed I have given you. I will then judge the plants that you bring, and the one I choose will be the next CEO."*
>
> *A man, named Jim, was there that day and he, like the others, received a seed. He went home and excitedly, told his wife the story. She helped him get a pot, soil and compost and he planted the seed.*
>
> *Jim kept checking his seed, but nothing ever grew. Three weeks, four weeks, five weeks went by, still nothing. By now, others were talking about their plants, but Jim didn't have a plant and he felt like a failure.*
>
> *Six months went by—still nothing in Jim's pot. A year went by and the CEO asked the young executives to bring their plants to work for inspection.*

When Jim told his wife that he wasn't going to take an empty pot, she asked him to be honest about what happened. When Jim arrived, he was amazed at the variety of plants grown by the other executives. They were beautiful—in all shapes and sizes. Jim put his empty pot on the floor and many of his colleagues laughed, a few felt sorry for him!

When the CEO arrived, he surveyed the room, "My, what great plants, trees and flowers you have grown," said the CEO. "Today one of you will be appointed the next CEO!"

The CEO spotted Jim at the back of the room with his empty pot. He asked Jim to come to the front of the room. The CEO asked him what had happened to his seed. Jim told him the story. The CEO asked everyone to sit down except Jim. He looked at Jim, and then announced to the young executives, "Behold your next Chief Executive Officer — Jim!"

Then the CEO said, "One year ago today, I gave everyone in this room a seed. I told you to take the seed, plant it, water it, and bring it back to me today. But I gave you all boiled seeds; they were dead - it was not possible for them to grow.

"All of you have brought me trees and plants and flowers. You substituted another seed for the one I gave you. Jim was the only one with the courage, integrity and honesty to bring me a pot with my seed in it. Therefore, he will be the new Chief Executive Officer!"

The EGO's Life

Honesty is the best policy.
—Benjamin Franklin

Our capacity for self-deception stems from defensive ego needs. The ego has its own belief system. Here are a few life-supporting truths on the ego:

- It is always right and is easily offended.
- It must win at any cost.
- It never has enough. It always wants more.
- It is achievement-oriented with selfish ambition.
- It is not good with change and desires control.
- It needs to be recognized as special.
- It is never in the present, is fearful of the future, and dwells on the past.
- It dislikes self-sacrifice.

In the book *Merton's Palace of Nowhere: A Search For God through Awareness of the True Self,* James Finley, a former Trappist novice under Thomas Merton, wrote, "There is something in me that puts on fig leaves of concealment, kills my brother, builds towers of confusion, and brings cosmic chaos upon the earth. There is something in me that loves darkness rather than light, that rejects God and thereby rejects my own deepest reality as a human person made in the image and likeness of God."

Integrity is known as a moral virtue. Virtues are behavioral traits and habits that help us focus and strive for ideals. For example, a person who has developed the virtue of honesty is often referred to as an honest person because he or she tends to be truthful and honest in all circumstances. Through virtue we grow in grace, knowledge, and understanding.

The opposite of virtue is vice or sin. Vices are bad habits or immoral conduct. Examples of vices are slander, greed, laziness, revenge, lust, and pride. Vices yield to temptation. The more deep-rooted and habitual the vice, the harder it is to overcome. We may not even recognize vice as vice. It is deceptive within a culture that *masks* the chief vice—idolatry of self. My generation was known as the "me generation." We were labeled as narcissistic. The terms *self-realization* and *self-fulfillment* were more important than social responsibility.

Self-help books in the 1960s led to self-gratification in the 1970s and to just plain selfishness in the 1980s. This is a sweeping statement, but it has been described in history in this way by authors like Thomas Wolfe, who wrote expressing of that time in the 1980s, "I think every living moment of a human being's life, unless the person is starving or in immediate danger of death in some other way, is controlled by a concern for status." Self-knowledge and self-awareness of our sinfulness is a necessary phase in our spiritual journey.

Two Standards

At the beginning of my spiritual journey, I read *The Spiritual Exercises* by St. Ignatius. Be aware that the Holy Spirit tends to custom-choose saints, experiences, and events to help you begin transforming your life once you have expressed even the smallest desire to increase your belief in God.

The Spiritual Exercises is structured to "exercise" your spiritual muscles. These exercises are a training in faith. Like an athlete must train, spiritual training requires a commitment of time and perseverance. At first, it is similar to entering a new land or going back to the old land with fresh eyes and vision. Beginning any new endeavor is like an adventure. There may be a fear of the unknown, but I found that these exercises open doors of prayer, discovery, mystery, action, stillness, beauty, and silence. I encourage you, like, St. Ignatius, to keep a journal as you gain self-knowledge and insight into your spiritual exercising.

St. Ignatius of Loyola originally structured his *The Spiritual Exercises* as a four-week silent retreat for Jesuits in formation. Many years later, they were made available for everyone, and today, they are known as one of the best retreats for spiritual renewal, transformation, and awakening to the love and will of God.

The chapter on "The Meditation on Two Standards" was a big wake-up call for me. The familiar saying is, "I'll believe it when I see it." But for Ignatius Loyola, his vision of reality actually controlled his perception. He was known to say, "When I believe it, I'll see it." We all need vision. *The Spiritual Exercises* reveal a "life vision." It helps us define "What is life all about for me?" In the "Two Standards" exercise, Ignatius asks us to choose between two ways of life: the standard of Satan or the standard of Christ.

Once the choice is made, we will find ourselves in direct opposition to, and in conflict with, the other. Ignatius saw life as a battle between good and evil. As Christians, we believe that there is a spiritual war going on for control of our souls. Satan, or Lucifer, whose name means light bearer, was once a glorious angel, but through the disfigurement of sin, he is now a demon. Satan is real. He hates us. We must resist the lies he presents to our egos and remain strong in our faith. He is limited by God with what he can do, but he does his utmost to remove peace from our souls because he knows that God abides in peace and that in peace, God, through us, accomplishes great things.

Grace at Work

Praying with *The Spiritual Exercises* inspired me go to confession for the first time in fifteen years. In this sacrament, you are confessing to God through the priest. It is healing for the soul and reestablishes our character and integrity. That confession was one of the most grace-filled experiences of my life. The priest, Fr. William McCarthy of St. John the Baptist's parish in Quincy, Massachusetts, was a pastor and a saintly man. He initiated Fr. Bill's Place, a homeless shelter for mentally ill veterans and alcoholics. The shelter has grown to two facilities aiding all the homeless, including families.

Fr. Bill's Christlike presence gently guided me through the confession, which started and ended in tears. He carefully asked me questions about my life because I did not know what to say. I am sure he could "read souls," because he actually told me my sins. It was a cleansing experience. Like Adam and Eve's experience with God, there was no more hiding. My soul and spirit were lifted. There was joy.

We are human. We will always sin. But I found that with frequent access to this sacrament, my awareness of sin gradually increased. My conscience became more enlightened. My selfishness began to take a back seat. I become more aware of others. Suddenly, I needed to help more. Love more. That is what *grace* does in any sacrament. It helps to overcome the ego and clear the way for the soul to give of itself. I broke up with my boyfriend not long after that significant confession. We had gone out for three years. I had come to realize that though I cared a great deal for him, I was not in love with him.

My sister and I moved back to Quincy nearer to my parents because of the long commute. The following year, we bought a house. A few months after my confession, I was reading the book *The Imitation of Christ*, which I learned about in St. Thérèse's *The Story of a Soul*. One night while reading, the idea of daily Mass was presented. My soul stirred, and my immediate response was, "Lord, this is too much to ask of me!" An hour or so later, I relented and made a deal with God. I said, "Lord, I am just going to do my usual thing in the morning, shower, not rush, and when I pass St. Ann's Church on my way to Interstate 93, if the time is right, I will go."

I took my time the next morning, got into my car, and when I reached St. Ann's church, I was stopped at a red light. People were walking in front of the car to go to Mass. I looked at my dashboard clock and saw that it was 6:55 a.m. So I pulled into the parking lot, self-consciously went into the church, and chose a seat. I was amazed at how many people went to daily Mass. The priest started Mass by saying, "Today is the Feast Day of St. Thérèse of Lisieux." It was October 1. I was shocked but had to smile. It seemed that St. Thérèse had decided to take me on and had become a patron saint. I went to 7:00 a.m. Mass every weekday after that but kept it a secret from family and friends.

About a year after I began attending daily Mass, I had brunch with my best friend. She was talking about her work, and I said, "You do such good. You have a beautiful, healing vocation." She was an occupational hand therapist at Brigham and Women's Hospital in Boston. Actually, she headed up the department. I told her, "Something is missing in my life. I want to help people. I do not have a vocation. I'm just making money and having a good time."

She said, "Go find something to do!" So, I began investigating what interested me. I started by training as a Red Cross instructor. Then, I looked into volunteering at St. Francis House, a day shelter in Boston, and took on kitchen duty one

Saturday a month. I found a three-year vocational prayer and began praying it every day.

One morning before 7:00 a.m. Mass, one of the priests came up behind me and asked if I would join the CCD (Confraternity of Christian Doctrine) teachers' group and teach one of the confirmation classes. I was volunteering, developing my prayer life, and attending daily Mass, but it was not enough. I felt there was more I needed to do. Looking back, I can see that there were desires in me and in my soul that I needed to identify and explore.

SIX
The Believer

THE LAND OF
FORGETFULNESS

Our birth is but a sleep and a forgetting.
—William Wordsworth

T he "sin of forgetfulness" was coined by one of the most famous women mystics this world has known—Julian of Norwich. An anchorite in the Middle Ages, Julian wrote *Revelations of Divine Love or (Showings)* in the 1400s. In this first book, written in English by a woman, she writes her well-known declaration of hope: "All shall be well, and all shall be well, all manner of things shall be well."

The sin of forgetfulness is a sin of blindness, which is a lack of sight and awareness of God's presence. She writes, "Because our spiritual eye is so blind, and we are so burdened with the weight of our mortal flesh ... we cannot see clearly the blessed face of our Lord God" and that "We are in God and He in us. We do not see." Our *memory* has the capacity to remember, as St. Augustine in his work, *De Trinitate (On the Trinity)* relates, "Being the creation of God and bearing the image of God, the mind always retains a knowledge of its own nature as God's created image; and thus, it must possess a 'memory of God' which is indelible, however deeply hidden away."

One reason for our forgetting is portrayed beautifully in a poem by William Wordsworth called, "Ode on Intimations of Immortality from Recollections from Early Childhood." Here is an excerpt:

> Our birth is but a sleep and a forgetting;
> The Soul that rises with us, our life's Star,
> Hath had elsewhere its setting
> And cometh from afar;
> Not in entire forgetfulness,
> And not in utter nakedness,
> But trailing clouds of glory do we come
> From God, who is our home:
> Heaven lies about us in our infancy.

There is a true story of a mother who entered the nursery to hear her three-year-old little girl talking to her newly born brother in his cradle. She was leaning over and whispering into his ear, "I am forgetting ... I *need* to remember! Remind me again of how it was before you came down."

In Rabbi Noah Weinberg's first book, *What the Angel Taught You,* he writes, "According to the Talmud, before we were born, when we were safely ensconced in the comfort of the womb, we all had access to the ultimate search engine. God dispatches a personal angel to each and every soul in utero, who sits beside each and every one of us, and actually teaches us *all* the wisdom we will ever need to know on this planet. Everything."

According to this legend, just before we are born, this angel gives us a little tap between the nose and the upper lip, and everything we were taught is immediately forgotten. That is how we receive that small indentation in the skin beneath our noses, known as the *philtrum*. Interestingly, when we have forgotten something and suddenly remember where it is, like our car keys, we instinctively put our finger up to our lip and say, "Ah! Now I remember!"

The philtrum was the angel's personal way of leaving an important message behind. Rabbi Weinberg writes, "When you seek the truth and feel like the search may be a lost cause, just run your finger over your lips, close your mouth, and feel the 'impression' that was made on you. Do not despair. You'll recognize reality when you see it. After all, you already found and understood it before."

This "impression" has been called the "brand of God" by Bernard Lonergan, "the kiss of God" by Ronald Rolheiser, and "the dark memory" by Henri Nouwen. Each of these theologians of our time talk of a primordial tender memory of "knowing" God. Rolheiser writes in his wonderful book *Wrestling with God: Finding Hope and Meaning in Our Daily Struggles to Be Human,* "Bernard Lonergan … suggests that a human soul does not come into the world as a *tabla rasa,* a pure, clean sheet of paper onto which anything can be written. Rather, for him, *we are born with the brand of the first principles indelibly stamped inside our souls.*" What does he mean by this?

In traditional theology and philosophy, there are four things called transcendental. They are oneness, goodness, beauty, and truth. Although everything that exists somehow bears these four qualities, they are perfect *solely* in God. Only God is *perfect* oneness, truth, goodness, and beauty. However, for Lonergan, God brands these four things, in their perfection, into the core of the human soul. "Hence, we come into the world already knowing, however dimly, perfect oneness, perfect truth, perfect goodness, and perfect beauty because they already lie inside us like an unerasable brand. Thus, we can tell right from wrong because we already know perfect truth and goodness in the core of our souls, just as we also instinctively recognize love and beauty because we already know them in a perfect way, however darkly, inside ourselves."

Lonergan expounds that, in this life, truth is not learned; it is recognized. Love is not learned; it is recognized. We don't learn what goodness is; we recognize it. We recognize these qualities because we already possess them in the core of our souls. We have been taught by mystics that the human soul comes from God and that God kisses it as He places it into our body. Our soul then goes through life always vaguely remembering that pure, loving kiss. Subsequently, we measure all of life's loves and kisses against that primordial, tender kiss. We also bear a dark memory, as Henri Nouwen says, of once having been caressed by hands far gentler than we ever meet in this life.

But how can we remember? What do we need to do? *We need to search.* We may want to look at how we are spending our time right now on earth. Sadly, here is one thing we are involved with almost constantly.

Spending Time

The following are some of the smartphone statistics with accompanying sources from DIY GENIUS. This online information/teaching company presented this information on their website in February 2021.

- The average adult in the United States will spend three hours, forty-three minutes per day on their mobile devices. —eMarketer Study
- The average American now spends sixty hours on screens per week, including watching television and using smartphones and computers at home and at work. —Nielsen "US Digital Consumer Report"
- The typical smartphone user checks his or her smartphone every twelve minutes from when they wake up until they go to sleep. For young people below the age of twenty-one, he or she checks his or her phone every 8.6 minutes. —"A Decade of Digital Dependency Study"
- The average smartphone user will tap, swipe, or click his or her smartphone 2,617 times a day, while the top 10 percent do this about 5,427 times a day. —Dscout's "Mobile Touches Report"
- It is estimated that 40 percent of the American population is addicted to their smartphones. On top of this, 58 percent of men and 47 percent of women suffer from nomophobia, which is the fear of being without a smartphone. —*Psychology Today*

- One out of every four car accidents in the United States is caused by texting and driving. —Edgar Snyder and Associates
- A study has shown that as mobile phone use increases, so does anxiety and depression. —"The Relationship Between Addiction to Smartphone Usage and Depression"

What is interesting to me is that Steve Jobs, Apple's cofounder and former CEO, who created many of the devices that we've become addicted to, would not let his children use iPads in the house. Also, many of the children of CEOs in Silicon Valley tech companies are in Montessori schools, which do not have computers and electronic devices. Perhaps that is because they themselves were students: Jeff Bezos, founder of Amazon; Bill Gates, founder of Microsoft; Sergey Brin and Larry Page, founders of Google. Jimmy Wales, founder of Wikipedia, was not a student, but he sent his children to Montessori.

Why Montessori? The Montessori Education, according to their website,

- encourages children to explore their world and to understand and respect the life forms, systems, and forces of which it consists.
- emphasizes the development of self-expression, true self-reliance, and agility in interpersonal relationships.
- fosters an understanding of the child's role in his or her community, culture, and the natural world.
- offers opportunities for imaginative exploration leading to confident, creative self-expression.

There are simple ways to reinvest and prioritize our time to include activities that are nurturing for our minds, souls, and bodies. But first, you need to consider, evaluate, and make the decision to gradually limit your smartphone use. Here are a few suggestions that can be started almost immediately once you inform your friends and family of your time saving decision: Set times to check and answer your messages and emails each day. Use your "Do Not Disturb" modes. Secure a place for your phone. Leave it there. Power-down your Wi-Fi at a certain time each night.

When we consider this need for change in our lives, we may get discouraged. We may feel overwhelmed, and our hope may be shaken. We may feel that there is really no way out, but that would not be true. That would be forgetting the power and ever-abiding love of God.

God, the Father
Our Father.
My Father.
Your Father.

He gave you life.
Love Him. He loves you.
Call Him. He's waiting to hear from you.
Trust Him. He gives you your next breath.
Hope in Him. In Him, is "Home, Sweet Home."
—Poem 110

PART II

The Truth of Living Hope

SEVEN
The Beginner

BEGIN AGAIN ...

*Life is a school where you learn how to
remember what your soul already knows.*
—Anonymous

In a recent homily, one of our priests told us an incredible life-changing story about a woman he had spiritually directed. Rosemary was an ICU pediatric nurse at Massachusetts General Hospital. Her nine-year-old daughter had been diagnosed with cancer and was dying. She called a priest who came to administer the sacrament of the sick and give her Holy Communion. Just as he was about to give the Eucharist to her, he stopped and asked Rosemary if she would like to give her daughter Jesus. Rosemary then had a profound experience. As she gave her daughter Jesus in the Eucharist, she realized that she was giving her daughter to Jesus at the same time. A great sense of peace and love overflowed into her. Given that experience of God and the consolation she received, she decided to investigate becoming a hospital chaplain. Not long after the death of her daughter, Rosemary began her studies while still working as a nurse, and after receiving her master's degree, she became a chaplain. She was then reassigned by the hospital as a chaplain, full time, and counseled staff, patients, and families for the next twenty years. She was known to say of her experience, "I was given a gift, and it cannot be hidden."

Life has its series of new beginnings. Some are carefully planned, and others are totally unexpected. In a matter of minutes, our lives, which have been the same day in and day out, for years, are subject to radical change. Occasionally, these transformative events or a chance meeting may make us stop, reflect, and think about a new life question. I call these "what-if moments." But on the whole, these self-reflective moments may be rare unless we are taken by surprise or are forced into them. We see ourselves in the mirror every day, but rarely do we "look inside." It takes courage to be self-reflective, to ask ourselves questions that may make us think, change, or grow. One question may lead to the "how" of another.

Actually, our self-discovery is endless, but questions are important. They are the ways we open doors to self-discovery. That first door of the spiritual life is critical; it is the door of self-knowledge. The *inner* journey of the spiritual life always starts with self-reflection. One of many self-reflective questions to ask yourself is, "If I could change anything about my life right now, what would it be?" Take time to think about this deeply. Honestly. Carefully. Before you ask yourself this question, you may want to pray and ask your soul to answer.

Soul Journaling

As we enter into this self-reflective process, I recommend journaling as a way to capture your thoughts. I have been journaling for over twenty-five years. I bought my first journal at a flea market for one dollar. It is still my favorite! As a history buff, I will just mention a little about the location of this flea market.

When I was fourteen, right before starting high school, our family moved from South Boston to Quincy, Massachusetts. It was about a twenty-minute ride south, eight miles away. Our new house was a block from the ocean. The sea breezes were still blowing, but this time from Quincy Bay. The flea market was within the building of the former Squantum Naval Air Station, a World War II fighter-pilot training hanger. This hanger was on a larger area of land on Quincy's waterfront, which is called Marina Bay today. Earlier in time, from 1927 to 1940, this section of Quincy was home to Dennison Airport. A social worker who lived in the neighboring area practiced her flying at this airport. Her name was Amelia Earhart.

During World War l, Victory Shipyard was also located on this oceanfront location. At one point, those shipyard workers created a ship in just forty-five days, setting a record for quick craft construction. But back to the 1970s. That flea market was huge. It would take days to go through all the stalls and tables of high- and low-priced jewelry, new and used books, beautiful antiques, and just plain good old stuff! I went to this flea market only once. It was with my mom, and I was probably around sixteen years old.

My mom entered the huge, wide-open doors and went in one direction, looking for antiques. At some point, I wandered away from her side and was perusing aimlessly, heading in the direction of the books. I was not looking for a journal, but the beauty of the cover stopped me. It was cobalt blue with a gold fleur-de-lis-like design on both sides. It was thin and had a cobalt-blue embossed ribbon binding. It was very beautiful and was only one dollar. I bought it not knowing what I would use it for. When I began to journal, which was about twenty years later, I bought a big black thick one that I marked up, underlined, and wrote in with abandon. I copied out segments of spiritual learnings from my readings. I wrote of hopes, frustration, and fears, nightly dreams and daily occurrences, and of family, friends, and life experiences. But the blue one with the fleur-de-lis, I saved for something special.

When I was thirty-seven, I transcribed my first poems in the beginning pages and then began to use it as a religious discernment journal. The last page's entry was the night before I entered the Carmelite Monastery in Boston. An interesting, soul-stirring facet to all this is that when we enter the monastery, we begin as a *postulant*. One year later, we enter the *novitiate*. As novices, we are "clothed" in the Carmelite habit, given a religious name and title, and receive a "symbol." We can submit three choices for our new religious names and titles to the prioress, but the symbol is a mystery. It is something given to us. The symbol I received was the fleur-de-lis.

Visioning

Fill your paper with the breathings of your heart.
—William Wordsworth

At the beginning of this vocation journey, as I began to read my spiritual books—which was usually at night—I grew in my trust that what I was reading was exactly God's communication to me for that time in my life. God leads us all individually. Personally. Trust opens the way to this relationship. Even though this time was actually a form of prayer, I did not recognize it as such. I saw it as growing in knowledge of the spiritual life. It was a new path with a new horizon. I was walking step-by-step in a faith adventure, alone with God, with great hope. And every night I found beauty, peace, and wonder. A new life was budding in me. I looked forward to that special time every evening. It was my secret time. And love and knowledge were growing.

What really surprised me was that I also began to write poetry. I needed to express creatively what I was feeling in addition to what I was learning. It just came out of me. Typically, this took place very late at night, after I had journaled my day's events and read a little. When we write for ourselves, freely and spontaneously, our consciousness is changed and our souls' thoughts rise to the surface. We may not even be aware at the time the pen is on the paper or the keys are being struck on the laptop. There is a connection taking place within our brains and minds that—when practiced— leads to deeper experiences of intuition, visualization, and creativity. In the process, journaling becomes a form of meditation. In particular, at night, the thoughts we have right before we sleep sink deeply into our subconscious, which is very active as we sleep. These thoughts germinate, resulting in peace, knowledge, and greater awareness of God's light reverberating in our souls.

You can journal on a computer, iPad, or laptop, but I suggest writing by hand in a paper journal, which has a stronger hand-heart-soul connection. As you begin to journal, allow your hand to write freely and just let go and let the thoughts flow. Forget spelling or making mistakes and just keep writing. You can certainly do this quicker on a computer, but a written journal will help to slow you down. It encourages a greater level of intimacy and more physical control. It helps you process what you are writing and gives your eyes a break from a sterile white screen, which may disturb your sleep, especially if you use one at night. Looking at your own handwriting may have more emotional impact than viewing your text on an impersonal computer device. Known as a therapeutic release, journaling is emotionally and mentally good for us. It stills us. It helps us to understand ourselves and our souls.

After answering your first question, "If I could change anything in my life right now, what would it be?" Another very good prompt to give yourself is, "If I had only one year to live, I would ..."

List thirty things as you begin your "I would" list. Write swiftly as the ideas come to you—don't think. You can use these prompts or make up your own: "I would like to." "I would try to," "I would hope to," "I would be ..."

Now, review the list and take time to ponder the question again. Pray and ask your soul, "Help me to see. Help me to understand." Write those final thoughts on your list and label them the "soul thoughts." Date it. This is not a bucket list or a wish list or a dream list. It is a vision list.

An example of a vision list might include the following:

- I would like to develop deeper relationships with my children.
- I would try to react from a loving perspective when in initial anger or fear.
- I would try to be more aware and appreciative of my daily blessings from God.
- I would like to appreciate the beauty of nature by spending more time outside.
- I would like to nurture my faith and grow in hope and surrender.
- I would like to try being kinder and more patient.
- I would like to learn to meditate.
- I would like to smile more.
- I would like to look for opportunities to help others.

In 2007, Reuters news agency reported the story of a single man who was told by his doctors that he had one year to live. He decided to radically change his life. He gave away and sold many of his possessions and decided to do only what would make him happy. At the end of the year, his doctors reviewed his diagnosis and apologized to him. They had been wrong. But he was not upset with his choices; he realized that during the previous year, he had successfully put his priorities in order, simplified his life, and he was much more fulfilled following his own encouraging dreams and simple desires.

The Spiritual Brain

O ur beliefs coupled with our desires are powerful change agents. Both are emotional energy directed by our brains, minds, and souls. Our minds, as consciousness, are beyond our brains and related directly to our souls. Our minds are self-conscious, thinking, knowing, loving, and willing. Our minds hold thought, emotion, determination, memory, and imagination. Interestingly, damage to our brains can modify our perceptual experiences, cognitive abilities, and personalities. However, as near-death experiences and neuroscience verify, our minds as pure consciousness continue to function even when the brain is severely damaged or clinically dead.

Neurotheology, also known as spirituality research, has been defined as an exploration of how the mind and brain operate in regard to one's relationship with God. In the past, spirituality had been excluded from scientific investigations as too mystical or transcendent for researchable attention. Christians were very private and were very resistant to being under the systematic study of their faith, beliefs, and prayer practices.

However, in 2008, Mario Beauregard, PhD, a neuroscientist— currently affiliated with the Department of Psychology at the University of Arizona—cowrote the book *The Spiritual Brain: A Neuroscientist's Case for the Existence of the Soul.* Drawing upon research with twenty-two Carmelite nuns, aged twenty-two to sixty-four, the study showed that during a deeply prayerful experience, their brains displayed signs of a very complex interaction with something distinct from themselves.

The main objective of this study was to measure electroencephalogram (EEG) spectral power in Carmelite nuns during a mystical experience. An EEG test detects electrical activity in your brain using electrodes that are attached to your scalp. Brain cells communicate through electrical impulses and are active all the time, even when you're asleep. This activity expresses itself as wavy lines on an EEG recording.

Before the beginning of the experiment, the Carmelites told him, "God cannot be summoned at will!" However, during the interviews conducted at the end of the experiment and documented in *The Spiritual Brain,* several nuns mentioned that they felt "the presence of God, His unconditional and infinite love, as well as plenitude and peace. They also felt a surrendering to God."[2] In conclusion, the study found actual brain-wave changes, which implicated several areas of the brain in both hemispheres. Increased *theta* waves and enhanced *alpha* connectivity were reported and documented during the mystical experiences at the time of the experiments.

What does this mean? Our brains are very interesting. They are like computers and are made up of billions of specific cells, called neurons. Neurons are constantly talking to each other, and the electrical activity that emanates from that communication can be detected and recorded as waves. In neuroscience, there are five different brain-wave frequencies, which are called beta, alpha, theta, delta, and gamma. Recognizing and exploring deeper states of consciousness will help to reveal the world of our subconscious minds, our souls.

Every brain-wave frequency has its own level of activity and unique state of consciousness:

---

[2] Mario Beauregard and Vincent Paquette, "Neural Correlates of a Mystical Experience in Carmelite Nuns," in *Neuroscience Letters 405* (Amsterdam: Elsevier, 2006), 186–190.

- Beta: Problem-solving, alert consciousness, thinking excitement, inner critic
- Alpha: Relaxing and recharging, creative, and artistic gateway to the subconscious
- Theta: Dreaming, imagination, inspiration, intuition, spiritual subconsciousness
- Delta: Deep, dreamless sleep, deep meditation, your unconscious mind
- Gamma: Intense concentration, heightened perception, bursts of insight

Brain waves change throughout the day and are influenced by what we're doing, thinking, and feeling at any given time. They are affected even while we sleep. The study with the Carmelite nuns indicated heightened activity within the theta and alpha brainwave frequencies. Let us take a better look at those states of consciousness.

Alpha is a state of calm and easing for the brain. Generally, the mind is focused on the here and now. Anytime you are in an act of refreshment and peace, you are in an alpha state. This state is relaxed and open to new possibilities. It is contemplative. It is a state of experiencing Kairos time. You reach this state by stopping and taking a rest, daydreaming, exercising, and through activities like watching TV, walking in a garden, or looking at the beauty in nature. Alpha waves are very important in that they boost creativity and reduce depression.

The theta brainwave state follows the alpha. It is the border between the conscious and subconscious world. This very-relaxed state slows the body down and helps it to heal, relieve stress, and enter into a deeper sleep state. The mind within theta activity experiences great intuition, profound creativity, and intense visualizations. It receives insights and inspiration beyond normal conscious awareness. Theta is the land of innovation for inventors and scientists. It is also the horizon for experiences of God.

I found it very interesting that theta is the main brainwave frequency for children, especially those between two and six years. In a sense, it explains Dado. However, adults who meditate and practice yoga also experience increases in alpha and theta brain activity. Taking time to rest and "be still" will increase the time of healthy brainwave activity within these states and will actually structurally change our brains and bodies. Healthy blood pressure, lowered stress levels, and deeper sleep patterns all have positive effects on our ways of living.

When we journal, reflect, or visualize changing our lives, we begin in an alpha state and then move importantly to theta. In theta, we strengthen our resolve, deepen our beliefs, and build upon new ideas without fear. We also access our souls. We receive inspiration and guidance from God.

EIGHT
The Beginner

BREATHE DEEP, FROM YOUR SOUL

Every breath I take
From You,
I give back to You,
With all my love.

—Poem 64

U nconsciously, we take over twenty-five thousand breaths a day. Our first breaths took place at our births, and our last will be at the moment of our deaths. Ancient religions see this breath of ours as God's, as stated by Genesis (2:7), when God breathed "the breath of life" into Adam's nostrils.

How we breathe effects our lives in ways we never imagined. Physically, breathing is divided into two distinct stages: *inspiration* (inhalation) and *expiration* (exhalation). When you breathe in, air enters your lungs, and oxygen from that air moves from your lungs into your blood. At the same time, carbon dioxide moves from your blood to the lungs and is breathed out. Utilizing 20 percent of that oxygen, your brain also gets involved. It receives signals from your body, detecting the amounts of oxygen and carbon dioxide in your blood, and sends signals to your muscles, adjusting your breathing rate depending on how active you are. If you are active, your breathing can increase up to about forty to sixty times a minute. When we rest or are asleep, it lowers to twelve to twenty times. Problem breathing can lead to decreased oxygen in the bloodstream, resulting in complications like headaches and, more severely, even to heart- and brain-functioning problems.

In his book *Breath: The New Science of a Lost Art,* author James Nestor, a science journalist plagued by recurring pneumonia and bronchitis, took a breathing class at his physician's recommendation, and describes the dramatic changes to his life as a result. "I talked to a neuropsychologist … and he explained to me that people with anxieties or other fear-based conditions typically will breathe way too much … putting yourself into a state of stress. Taking 'slow and low' breaths *through the nose* can help relieve stress and reduce blood pressure." Our noses perform multiple functions in our bodies, and amazingly, it even helps to keep us *balanced.*

Deep diaphragmatic breathing, also known as slow abdominal breathing, affects our blood by depositing it into the thoracic cavity and shooting it back out throughout the body, producing a calm and relaxed feeling in the *mind* and in the *entire* body. Long, deep breaths also improve heart-rate variability, the measurement of variations within beat-to-beat intervals. Many of us, when anxious or stressed, have heard friends and family say, "Take a deep breath. Everything will be okay!" Well, physiologically, hearing and doing this does help! But take that breath through your nose. It has been proven that we receive 20 percent more oxygen by breathing and exhaling through our noses than through our mouths. This is very important for healthy deep sleep.

Doctors and scientists are now investigating deep breathing, especially through the nose, as a new healing science. There are many breathing books, techniques, and classes available. I encourage you to research them for your general well-being and to enhance your prayer life.

Breath Praying

Be still, and know that I am God.
                                   —Psalm 46:10

Author James Nestor not only learned about the physical effects of deep breathing, but the spiritual benefits as well. He experienced a conversion at his breathing class that led him to lifelong change. He was not conscious of any immediate transformation taking place, but he did feel as if he had been taken from one place and moved into another, calmer realm.

Spiritually and mystically, deep breathing has been the foundation for prayer for centuries for Yogis, Tibetan Buddhists, Desert Fathers and Mothers, and Orthodox monks and nuns William Johnston, an Irish Jesuit internationally renowned for his work on mysticism and interfaith dialogue, wrote in his book, *Christian Zen*: "Breath rises from the very root of the being, so that consciousness of the breath can lead to a realization of the deepest self by opening up new doors ... the rhythm of breath leads to something deeper." This rhythm of breath will point to the cores of our beings, that divine spark, which is the true self, the realm from which our souls awaken.

Ancient breathing meditation practices, such as the prayer of the heart or Jesus prayer, Qigong, Tai chi, Tummo, and Pranayama breathing are all related to praying to the rhythm of breaths. The Hail Mary, as part of the rosary, is also a rhythmic breathing prayer. This scripturally based contemplative prayer brings us to meditate on the mysteries of Jesus's life using, primarily, repetitions of the Hail Mary, (the Aves). In my last years at Polaroid, I worked in consumer marketing heading up a product group responsible for all US camera, film, and accessory sales. Daily life was a series of constant phone calls and emails, not to mention scheduled and impromptu meetings. After work, I literally unplugged myself from phone and email. To unwind every night, I would walk four miles along the beach and pray using a rosary ring. That meditative prayer calmed me and stilled my soul. The combination of prayer, the beauty of nature, and exercise brought me to a level of peace and surrender that sustained me in that enjoyable, yet very demanding time in my professional life.

When prayer is aligned to our very breathing, it becomes "breath prayer." Breath prayer has origins in the lives of the Desert Fathers and Mothers; it is a way to "pray without ceasing," and it brings our consciousness into the presence of God. The most well-known Christian breath prayer, the Jesus prayer, also known as the prayer of the heart, is very simple but requires perseverance and discipline. This Orthodox prayer is powerful in that the name of Jesus is repeated over and over hundreds of times a day: Lord, Jesus Christ, Son of God, have mercy on me, a sinner.

The Jesus prayer, which is very old and was recommended by the church fathers, was made famous by the classic book *The Way of a Pilgrim*. This nameless Russian autobiography details the author's travels across his country while practicing the Jesus prayer with the help of a prayer rope and the study of the *Philokalia*, a spiritual text for contemplation. The prayer practice can be simplified to just repeating Jesus's name. To do this, you should breathe in through your nose, silently praying, *Je*, and then out through your mouth, praying, *sus*. The power in Jesus's name to provide grace, hope, and healing is beyond our understanding. This prayer can be prayed anywhere, anytime. It can be used in times of stress or fear, at a moment of needed patience, or as your daily meditation.

Commenting on this way of praying, one of the most prominent Orthodox saints, Theophan the Recluse, states, "The essential part is to dwell in God, and this walking before God means that you live with the conviction ever before your consciousness that God is in you, as He is in everything: you live in the firm assurance that He sees all that is within you, knowing you better than you know yourself. This awareness of the eye of God looking at your inner being must not be accompanied by any visual concept but must be confined to a simple conviction or feeling."

The *Breath Prayer* activates our souls and aligns them to our bodies. The Holy Spirit breathes through us, in us, and with us. This uniting of breath with our prayers is another way of "praying always"—a way of being present to God, very simply, in the here and now.

I recommend journaling your experience of this powerful prayer.

1. Find a special place to pray—a place of solitude, silence, beauty, and peace.
2. Close your eyes and be still, opening yourself before the presence of God.
3. Now imagine that God is calling you by name and asking you, "What is it you seek?"
4. Give God a simple and direct answer that comes honestly from your spiritual desires. No need to think; respond spontaneously. Record your request by writing it down. Your request may be several words or a phrase such as, "Help me to know you," "Help me to surrender," "Increase my desire for you," or "Show me the way." Or you may use a simple word, like "peace, strength, joy, or love." Whatever you are

seeking, these words are the basis for your breath prayer.

5. Now, use the name with which you are most comfortable when speaking to God. Combine it with your written request to the question God asked you. This is your prayer.

6. Breathe in the first phrase or word, and breathe out the second phrase. Breathe in, *Jesus*; breathe out, *I trust in you.*

In time, it will become natural to pray this way throughout the day. Subconsciously, I have woken up in the middle of the night with my prayer words on my lips. For years, I prayed to Jesus, "I love you, Lord. You are my strength"—a variation from Psalm 18:1. Another favorite is, "Your kingdom come. Your will be done" (Matthew 6:10). As you progress with this prayer, especially in meditation, take longer deep breaths: inhale for five seconds, hold for five seconds, and exhale for five seconds. Deeper breaths at night before bed will relax you, and you will fall asleep faster and have a more refreshed night sleep.

Consciously breathing in God, our souls are at rest. Our lives are full of peace because we recognize that we live, move, and have our beings in Him. Our desire that we remain in God and that God remain in us makes our lives a loving adventure of trust, hope, and love. Even as we go through the dark moments of our lives, we have built up trustful assurance that God is with us.

NINE
The Beginner

THE ETERNAL VIEW

*I have always believed, and I still believe,
that whatever good or bad fortune may come
our way, we can always give it meaning and
transform it into something of value.*
— Hermann Hesse, author of *Siddhartha*

There is a story about a young man who once approached Socrates and asked the philosopher how he could acquire wisdom and knowledge. "Follow me," Socrates said in response, as he led the young man down to the sea. The young man followed as Socrates began wading through the water, first at ankle depth, then knee, then waist, and finally, to shoulder height. Then, rather abruptly, Socrates grabbed the young man and dunked him under the water. The young man struggled desperately, and just before he blacked out, Socrates pulled him up.

Infuriated, the young man screamed, "What are you doing?! Trying to kill me?"

Calmly, Socrates responded, "Absolutely not. If that was my intention, I would not have pulled you up."

"Then why did you just do that?" the young man gasped.

"When you want wisdom and insight as badly as you desired that breath of air, then you shall have it," Socrates replied, looking the man in the eyes. Then he turned toward the shore and walked away.

Desires are like seeds that God has planted in us and that we need to activate. Spiritual desires are hidden and unknown to our egos but known by our souls. They are the buried treasure within us that must be discovered to fulfill who we are called to be. Desires and longings are signposts on a map to our inner selves. Certainly, there are universal desires, such as peace, happiness, and love, that all of us have. But within you are desires that are exclusively yours. They are eternal desires.

The Carmelite St. Thérèse of Lisieux said, "God would never inspire me with desires which cannot be realized; so, in spite of my littleness, I can hope to be a saint." Andrew and John, in their desire to know Jesus, asked Him, "Where are you staying?" (John 1:38). And Jesus responded those powerful, soul-stirring words, "Come and See" (John 1:39). "They went and saw the place Jesus was staying" (John 1:39). And their lives were forever changed.

Eternal desires within our souls change our lives. We "find ourselves." Our destinies.

THE BEGINNER

Re-Viewing Our Lives

To see, *really* see, has been called an art. It requires vision. It is not a simple looking. It is learned. Henry David Thoreau wrote, "It is not what you look at that matters, it is what you see."

Two people can look at the same scene and see it from a totally different perspective. A psychologist and an arresting officer may perceive the actions of a teen gang member from divergent viewpoints. One sees a troubled youth. Another sees a troublemaker. *Seeing* involves a greater understanding. More patience. A deeper awareness of love. Maybe that is why a person with the gift of wisdom, profound spiritual insight, and intuition is called a *seer*.

From the moment of our births, we are human *beings* who are seeing, learning, evaluating, and perceiving. We are becoming. In philosophy, *theoria* is a Greek word for "the way of seeing." It is directly connected to the Greek word *ethos*, "the way of being."

Being is awareness. The little "I am." Living in the present moment. Children simply are; they trust and take in everything around them. They are naturally contemplative. Becoming is an openness to moving forward, a conscious stepping into an unfolding plan, recognizing a new horizon and going toward it. Becoming leads to transcendence, going beyond who we are into new possibilities. Building on this potentiality. Seeing and living life another way. There is newness.

Becoming is related to seeking, asking questions of ourselves and others. Exploring the *whys*, *what-ifs*, and *hows*, and pondering them. Then it is moving into action with *expectation* and *hope*. Becoming is not a waiting to see what others think in a search for acceptance, affirmation, or praise.

— 65 —

Becoming is an inward journey moving outward. It is sought in silence and solitude, yet later expressed in remarkable ways before the world.

The concepts of *being* and *becoming* are philosophic, coming from the Greek word *philosophia*, which means "love of wisdom." Philosophy is a way of thinking about the world and the universe, which studies the questions and problems of reality and existence. Ideals, standards, or beliefs, used to describe behavior and thought, are included in the study of philosophy.

As human beings, we have our own philosophies on life. We live with principles, ideals, opinions, and dreams. As we age, or at critical times in our lives' journeys, we may stop and question ourselves about our own philosophies on life. We may look back to see where our past decisions, our motivations, and our dreams have taken us. Perhaps we need to take a little time to *re-view* ourselves from the beginning.

Jesus's "come and see" invitation to Andrew and John was to a new *theoria,* "way of seeing," as well as a new *ethos*, "way of being." Our Lord has extended this tender open invitation to all of us. We are the beloved of God from the very beginning, and there is no end. For we are on an eternal journey ...

Enjoy this beautiful poem by Rainer Maria Rilke, translated by Anita Barrows, in her book *Rilke's Book of Hours: Love Poems to God:*

Go to the Limits of Your Longing

God speaks to each of us as He makes us,
Then walks with us silently out of the night.

These are the words we dimly hear:

You, sent out beyond your recall,
Go to the limits of your longing.
Embody me.

Flare up like flame
And make big shadows I can move in.

Let everything happen to you: beauty and terror.
Just keep going. No feeling final.
Don't let yourself lose me.

Nearby is the country they call life.
You will know it by its seriousness.

Give me your hand.

The Divine Presence

When I was in my early thirties, Polaroid sent me to the Kellogg School of Management in Chicago. One beautiful October night, I was walking around the campus, and I came upon the university bookstore. I went directly to the business section but then moved on to the spirituality section and pulled *The Practice of the Presence of God* off the shelf. It is a classic book on Carmelite spirituality. Looking back, it was yet another sign of my Carmelite vocation. But I was just curious at that point. The book looked intriguing. I liked the title! And it was not too thick. Perfect reading for an intense course study time.

The Practice of the Presence of God is a contemplative form of prayer that is a practiced habit of "being with God." It is a daily lived awareness that God is everywhere, that we are in God, and, most importantly, that God is present within us.

The practice was made famous by a discalced Carmelite lay brother, Lawrence of the Resurrection (Nicolas Herman), who lived in France in the 1600s. A very simple man, Brother Lawrence was a cook and a sandal-repairer within the Carmelite monastery. Well known for his wisdom, his Maxims and letters were collected and edited and made available after his death, resulting in his spiritual masterpiece *The Practice of the Presence of God*. This book, a classic in spirituality, has universal appeal to people of all faiths.

Brother Lawrence writes, "God does not ask much of us, merely a thought of Him from time to time, a little act of adoration, sometimes to ask for His grace, sometimes to offer Him your sufferings, at other times to thank Him for the graces, past and present, He has bestowed on you, in the midst of your troubles to take solace in Him as often as you can."

This practice, over time, strengthens us in faith and hope, leading us to total trust and surrender. It is another way to "pray always," but more importantly, it moves us to enter into a love relationship with God. This was basically my relationship with Dado when I was a child. I babbled and shared everything with him. I was aware that he was always with me. He was my closest friend. I did not live my life without him.

One simple way to bring the awareness of Jesus into your life is a habit the Mother Teresa had and taught. Every morning, the very first thing she did when she got out of bed was to say, "Good morning, Jesus." This may seem too simple, but the consistency will change you over time. Your consciousness will gently awaken and begin to grow. I encourage you to try it for a few months to see what happens.

As Carmelites, we spend the first hour in solitary prayer with the Lord after we awaken. St. Teresa of Avila said, "Prayer is nothing else than an intimate sharing between friends: it means taking time frequently to be alone with Him whom we know loves us."

In the Book *He and I,* Jesus speaks to the mystic Gabrielle Bossis these gentle- yet slightly imploring words,

> Practice the presence of My love. I am everywhere. Put your head on My heart. Of course, since this pleases Me. If only you understood the gift of God and Who is speaking to you. Come to Me … I want to heal you of your weak faith, of your life lived apart from Me rather than in Me, of your shortsighted view of My actual Presence. Think 'My great friend, my Beloved is not absent. I cannot see Him or touch

Him, but He is there with His extravagance of love.'
Do you want this? Right away … Ceaselessly?

This way of prayer, as loving friendship with Jesus, is illustrated so beautifully in this true story from Brennan Manning's book: *Abba's Child: The Cry of the Heart for Intimate Belonging,* Navpress Publishing Group.

Once a woman asked me to come and pray with her father, who was dying of cancer. When I arrived, I found the man lying in bed with his head propped up on two pillows and an empty chair beside his bed. I assumed the old fellow had been informed of my visit.

"I guess you were expecting me," I said.

"No, who are you?"

"I'm the new associate at your parish," I replied. "When I saw the empty chair, I figured you knew I was going to show up."

"Oh yeah, the chair," said the bed-ridden man. "Would you mind closing the door?"

Puzzled, I shut the door. "I've never told anyone this, not even my daughter," said the man, "but all my life I have never known how to pray. At the Sunday Mass I used to hear the pastor talk about prayer, but it always went right over my head.

"I abandoned any attempt at prayer," he continued, "until one day about four years ago my best friend said to me, 'Joe, prayer is just a simple matter of having a conversation with Jesus. Here's what I suggest. Sit down on a chair, place an empty chair in front of you, and in faith see Jesus on the chair. It's not spooky because He promised, "I'll be with you all days." "Then just speak to Him and listen in the same way you're doing with me right now.'

"So, Padre, I tried it, and I like it so much that I do it a couple of hours every day. I'm careful, though. If my daughter saw me talking to an empty chair, she'd send me off to the funny farm."

I was deeply moved by the story and encouraged the old man to continue on the journey. Then I prayed with him, anointed him with oil, and returned to the rectory.

Two nights later, the daughter called to tell me that her father had died that afternoon.

"Did he seem to die in peace?" I asked.

"Yes. But there was something strange. In fact, beyond strange—rather weird. Apparently just before Dad died, he leaned over and rested his head on a chair beside his bed."

Prayer Spaces

Having a prayer space is very important in developing your soul's relationship with God. This is the place where you pray and speak with God. It is a mini-retreat site for you where you rest in God's presence, where you read, meditate, or pray the rosary. It can be a small corner in your bedroom or family room. It can be a special location outside of your home—a remote place in a park, in the woods, your garden, or on your deck. It is generally a place of solitude, silence, and stillness.

This prayer location can have a beautiful holy image, an icon, candle, or a crucifix. If it is located in a general area, you may find that other members of your family will use it too. Ultimately, God is in your soul, so every time you close your eyes and go within yourself, wherever you are, you are with Him.

TEN
The Learner

INTO THE DEEP MYSTERY

There is a place deep inside, where one's real
life goes on, much like an underground river
in a parched, dry, country, which flows,
whether one knows about it or not.
—Sharon Butala, *The Perfection of the Morning*

When we set out to "be with God" we are entering into mystery. The unknown. Ourselves. Classically, in spirituality, we are triggering our minds, memories, and wills. These are the three powers of the soul. In essence, our "being." Over the courses of our lives, we pack and carry a lot of emotional baggage. We have scars from our experienced sufferings, losses, betrayals, and the everyday wounds of life. No one escapes them. These are the dark shadows of our pasts. Some experiences may still be unresolved. Some relationships may still be unforgiven.

At the extreme, life can become "frozen in time," a series of reruns and replays. We retreat into hiding. Wounds of abuse, neglect, and trauma may be so deep that they are repressed, or consciously unknown. But the soul remembers everything. Anytime we feel severe stress and are unable to change our circumstances, for whatever reason, our nervous systems are affected and become overwhelmed, and our abilities to cope fails. We freeze in a way that our fears are locked into our bodies, leading to chronic anxiety, depression, and addictions. The most painful layer of suffering that surrounds us may be a sense of shame. We may move on, but the problems continue to live deep inside us, affecting how we relate to God, others, and ourselves in ways that we may not realize. The process of recovery is to awaken self-compassion and reconnect with our souls in that lost, sacred sense of the Spirit.

> *The wound is where light enters you.*
> —Rumi

People battling cancer or walking on crutches receive immediate encouragement, help, and empathy. However, the emotional wounds from trauma, heartbreak, abandonment, and abuse are invisible. Unrecognized. Youth, in a particular way, need help. Suicide is the second leading cause of death among young people within the ages of ten to twenty-four. The rate of suicide with this group rose 60 percent between 2007 and 2018, according to a report released in September 2020 by the Centers for Disease Control and Prevention. Drug addiction, bullying, and abuse are a few of the major factors leading to youth suicide.

Suicide impacts the whole family. Everyone experiences severe trauma with that form of sudden death. Research from behavioral medicine and health psychology are revealing that both emotional pain and physical pain register in the same place in our brains. These wounds are very real.

Trauma is a Greek word for injury. We all experience trauma at some point in our lives. Healing will take time and effort. It is essential that this pain is acknowledged and embraced before you can move on. Hope is a crucial factor in the nurturing of healing transformation. One small glimmer of hope can open the locked doors of our sorrow and pain and allow them to be perceived in a new way of understanding. It can change the way we look at the past and our present reality.

And hope is felt. Our bodies feel hope. It is an energy that sustains us in the challenges of recurring depression, anxiety, and feelings of loss. Hope is not tangible. You can't see it, but the effects of hope, like the effects of faith and love, are a source of strength, peace, and joy that are God-given. Hope is a gift from our God. It anchors the soul. It is the soul's way of awakening and healing battered and frozen emotions and going forward into a future with renewed trust.

This beginning stage of awakening healing is poignantly portrayed in the children's book *The Secret Garden*. Lord Craven is a wounded man who has painfully locked himself away for years, grieving the death of his young wife. His wife had a beautiful gated rose garden that, in his suffering, he had locked. Hence the book's title. After ten years, he is on a solitary trip abroad walking in a beautiful valley, and he stops. "The valley was very, very still. As he sat gazing into the clear running of the water, Archibald Craven gradually felt his mind and body both grow quiet, as quiet as the valley itself. He wondered if he were going to sleep, but he was not. He sat and gazed at the sunlit water and his eyes began to see things growing at its edge."[3]

Contemplation is a form of seeing. Brother Lawrence of the Resurrection, called contemplation "the loving gaze that finds God everywhere." This gazing requires stillness and solitude where the contemplative mind openly receives, is present to the moment, to the now, without judgment or analysis. It is a kind

---

[3] Frances Hodgson Burnett, *The Secret Garden* (New York: Barnes and Noble Classics, 2005), 216.

of letting go. A resting in God, beyond words, beyond thoughts, beyond activity.

St. John of the Cross called contemplation, "nothing other than a secret, peaceful, loving inflow of God."

"There was one lovely mass of blue forget-me-nots growing so close to the stream that its leaves were wet and at these he found himself looking as he remembered he had looked at such things years ago. He was actually thinking tenderly how lovely it was and what wonders of blue its hundreds of little blossoms were."[4]

Remembering is a pulling together of thoughts from our past, returning in memory to our *beginning* places that hold particular times of discovery and wonderful experiences of joy, beauty, and peace. "He did not know that just that simple thought was slowly filling his mind—filling and filling it until other things were softly pushed aside. It was as if a sweet clear spring had begun to rise in a stagnant pool and had risen and risen until at last, it swept the dark water away."[5]

Archibald's soul was nurturing his mind, healing and awakening his consciousness to a time before the trauma. This contemplation was happening in *Kairos* time with *theta* brain waves. It was a healing experience of God in nature.

"He did not know how long he sat there or what was happening to him, but at last he moved as if he were awakening and he got up slowly and stood on the moss carpet, drawing a long, deep, soft breath, and wondering at himself. Something seemed to have been unbound and released in him, very quietly. 'What is it?' he said, almost in a whisper, and he passed his hand over his forehead. 'I almost feel as if—I were alive!'"[6]

---

4 Burnett, *The Secret Garden*, 216.

5 Burnett, *The Secret Garden*, 217.

6 Burnett, *The Secret Garden*, 217.

The secret of *The Secret Garden* is that transformation, healing, and growth take place in hidden, unknown spaces within you that seem to be dead. Locked away. Imprisoned. The two main characters in this story are Colin, Lord Craven's neglected and apparently crippled son, and his orphaned ten-year-old cousin, Mary, who had recently come to live with them from India. Mary is difficult. Spoiled by house staff and neglected by her parents, she is totally self-centered. One day, while Lord Craven is traveling, she finds the rusted hidden key to the secret garden that he had used to lock it ten years before, and she enters in.

> She thought she saw something sticking out of the black earth—some sharp little pale green points ... she knelt down to look at them.
>
> "Yes, they are tiny growing things and they might be crocuses or snowdrops or daffodils," she whispered. "Perhaps there are some other ones coming up in other places," she said. "I will go all over the garden and look."
>
> Mary went slowly and kept her eyes on the ground. She looked on the old border beds and among the grass, and after she had gone round, trying to miss nothing, she had found ever so many sharp, pale green points, and had become quite excited again.
>
> "It isn't a quite dead garden," she cried out softly to herself.
>
> Hope was springing up in her. Mary didn't know anything about gardening, but the grass seemed so thick in some places where the green points were pushing their way through that she thought they did not seem to have enough room to grow. She searched about and found a rather sharp piece of

wood and knelt down and dug and weeded until she made nice clear places around them."

"Now they look as if they could breathe," she said, after she had finished with the first ones.

"I am going to do ever so many more."[7]

---

[7] Burnett, *The Secret Garden*, 67.

Our Secret Garden

We all have a secret garden within ourselves that we have locked away from the world's view and perhaps from our own consciousness. Your secret garden may be

- Hopes and dreams that have been shelved, put aside, and neglected.
- Painful experiences of childhood.
- The creative inclinations within us that are undeveloped.
- The hoped-for places to which we never traveled.
- The friends who have slipped away.
- The areas of our consciences that need forgiveness and healing.
- The relationships that need to be reconciled.
- The need for time to ourselves—to breathe again and to bloom in new and different ways.

Only you can answer the questions related to your secret garden. Ponder this idea and take time to journal your answers. Do this exercise in a place of beauty. Pray before you begin. Ask your soul to open the door to that gated garden. However, some deeply painful experiences and trauma needing "forgiveness and healing" may require assistance from a counseling professional and should not be opened by this exercise.

Nature Heals

Nature-based therapeutics focuses on the healing effects of nature, be it wilderness recovery programs, hug-a-tree parks, nature walks, forest therapy, healing gardens, or just sitting by the ocean. Nature heals and soothes us through many senses: listening to nature sounds as we fall asleep, watching a sunset or the ongoing waves break on the shore, digging up the earth and planting flowers or vegetables. These are all soul-stirring times of refreshment and peace. We need these times, physically and psychologically. Nature retunes our minds and bodies.

There have been many studies on nature aiding the recovery process in hospitals. Patients whose windows faced trees or a garden, rather than a brick wall or a sterile environment, recovered fasted and needed fewer painkillers. The *Journal of Attention Disorders*, in an article in 2009, showed that children with attention deficits concentrate better after a walk in a park. Dr. Nooshin Razani, MD, directs the Center for Nature and Health at UCSF Benioff Children's Hospital in Oakland, California. She treats her patients with type-2 diabetes, depression, anxiety, and feelings of loneliness and isolation with "nature prescriptions."

In her TED Talk, *Prescribing Nature for Health*, she related to her audience the following:

"Let's say, for example, you go into a forest. Within minutes, your heart rate will come down, you will breathe slower, you sweat less, and cortisol, the stress hormone, starts decreasing."

"I routinely prescribe nature to children and families," says Razani. "Nature has the power to heal. It has the power to heal because it is where we are from, it is where we belong, and it belongs to us as an essential part of our health, and actually of our survival."

My father was diagnosed with inoperable lung cancer when I was twenty-eight. He was a master electrician who worked for E.G. Sawyer Company. Founded in 1864, E. G Sawyer is the nation's oldest continuously operated electrical contracting business. Growing up, I remember him working at Boston University, Harvard, Logan Airport, and being involved in the restoration of many old churches and buildings downtown. One of his favorites was Trinity Church. I used to say that my Dad "lit up" a lot of Boston! At fifty-eight, he was diagnosed with mesothelioma, asbestos poisoning. He was given three years to live but ended up with seven. Every other year, during his chemo treatment, was a good year. His oncologist taught at Harvard and practiced at Mass General. The news that changed my family's life forever took place over a dinner table.

Every six months, Dad would go to the hospital to be checked. My sister worked at the *Boston Globe*, and I was at Polaroid. We would wait for the call that would result in dinner at home or a celebration at a restaurant. In many ways, our lives revolved around my father's condition and support for my mom. It was always in the back of our minds that we were all living on borrowed time. To this day, if I think of my Dad, my eyes will fill with tears—tears of love and loss.

During his chemo years, he would remain in the hospital for one-week stretches. His doctor was involved in charting and testing varying new protocols and experimental treatments, and my dad's life was extended as he took part in many of these studies. Some were harsh. Others were easy. But he never complained. I remember going over to Mass General for lunch with him a few days a week. Polaroid headquarters was only two miles away over the Longfellow Bridge in Cambridge.

One of my strongest memories of that time was of the tree outside my office window that I would gaze at when I returned. My office was on the second floor beside a massive maple. I named it Ned. The office window was huge, almost floor to ceiling. So, Ned the tree filled a wall space. It was like having him inside my office with me. Anytime I was on the phone, putting out fires, or coming back from stressful meetings, I would close the door and gaze at Ned's solidity. He stilled me. Centered me. Gave me hope. He was timeless. He was so beautiful, coming alive in early spring, was lovely in summer, and was glorious in the fall. But I loved him most in winter when he was stripped of his leaves and vulnerable or glistening with snow-laden limbs. Ned's presence sustained me. And that tree "knew it." What is interesting is that the name Ned is a form of Edward. Edward G. Sawyer.

Maybe subconsciously, my soul was trying to help me forgive the company that did not adequately protect its electricians against asbestos poisoning. In addition to my dad, there were many others who died. Others had severe respiratory illnesses. There were a multitude of lawsuits. One Boston law firm approached all the victims. Edward G. Sawyer, who started the company, had long since gone home to God. During the investigations, it was discovered that the present company owners were aware of the dangers involved.

My mom has been, and still is, very well off financially. To this day, at ninety-one, she will say that losing my dad feels like yesterday and that half of her is gone. But I guess that testifies more—not to the healing power of forgiveness (although she has forgiven), but rather to the incredible power of their love.

ELEVEN
The Learner

LAUDATO SI

The universe unfolds in God, who fills it completely.
Hence, there is a mystical meaning
to be found in a leaf,
in a mountain trail, in a dewdrop,
in a poor person's face.
The ideal is not only to pass from
the exterior to the interior,
to discover the action of God in the soul,
but also, to discover God in all things.
—Laudato Si (223)

Two years into his pontificate, Pope Francis wrote his second encyclical *Laudato Si'* (*Praise Be to You*). *Laudate Si* states the need for us to look at our world through new *spiritual* eyes and to see that everything is interconnected and that all of creation is a "kind of universal family" with God as our Creator. Nature cannot be seen as something apart from humanity or merely the place where we live. Creation is of the order of love. God's love is the fundamental moving force in all created things.

The phrase *Laudate Si* is from Saint Francis of Assisi's "Canticle of the Sun," a poem in which God is praised for creation and for all creatures. St. Francis dictated the prayer/

poem at the end of his life, and at a time, he was blind. Father Eric Doyle, in his book, *St. Francis and the Song of Brotherhood and Sisterhood*, writes, "Though physically blind, he was able to see more clearly than ever with the inner eye of his mind. With unparalleled clarity, he perceived the basic unity of all creation …"

Canticle of the Sun

Most High, all powerful, good Lord,
Yours are the praises, the glory,
the honor, and all blessing.
To You alone, Most High, do they belong,
and no one is worthy to mention Your name.
Be praised, my Lord, through all your creatures,
especially through my lord Brother Sun,
who brings the day; and you give light through him.
And he is beautiful and radiant in all his splendor!
Of you, Most High, he bears the likeness.
Praised be You, my Lord, through Sister Moon
and the stars, in heaven you formed them
clear and precious and beautiful.
Praised be You, my Lord, through Brother Wind,
and through the air, cloudy and serene,
and every kind of weather through which
You give sustenance to Your creatures.
Praised be You, my Lord, through Sister Water,
which is very useful and humble
and precious and chaste.
Praised be You, my Lord, through Brother Fire,
through whom you light the
night and he is beautiful
and playful and robust and strong.
Praised be You, my Lord, through
Sister Mother Earth,
who sustains us and governs us and who produces
varied fruits with colored flowers and herbs.
—St. Francis of Assisi

Every year, there is mounting evidence that the natural world has a consciousness. Biologists, naturalists, ecologists, and foresters claim that trees can speak and that plants have intelligence. Books such as *The Hidden life of Trees: What they Feel, How They Communicate—Discoveries from a Secret World* and *What a Plant Knows* reveal studied behaviors that look like memory, decision-making, communication, and learning.

Plants *are* conscious, according to the International Laboratory of Plant Neurobiology director Stefano Mancuso, an arboriculture professor at the University of Florence. Mancuso's case for plant consciousness hinges on evidence that they are aware of their existence, of their surroundings, and of the passing of time. But it is not only the plant world that has memory. Ground-breaking research by Dr. Masaru Emoto shows water as a living entity, capable of thought and memory. Using photography, he documented changes in water at the molecular level when it is exposed to music, thought, and intent. Every drop had a unique face that was clearly visible in its frozen crystal form. He concluded that water is deeply connected to our consciousness, individually and collectively.

I found that animals have a deeper consciousness than we realize. Our dog, Chelsea, was devoted to my dad. Every night, she would lay at the foot of my father's hassock as he read the paper or watched TV in his den. When my dad died, she no longer crossed the threshold into that room. Three years later, in the last months of her life, she was unable to go up the stairs to the second floor, where the bedrooms and den were located. One afternoon, my mom could not find her. Looking outside and everywhere on the first floor, she finally went upstairs and found her in the den right by the hassock where she always rested by my dad. She looked at my mom, and my mom started crying and called our vet, who took Chelsea and put her to sleep two hours later. Our vet loved Chelsea and later called my mom and said her passing was very peaceful and pain-free. He held her the whole time. Back then, you could not be present at a pet's passing. How Chelsea got up those stairs we do not know, but she knew what she was doing.

Native American Spirituality

Native American and Celtic spiritualities are particularly sensitive to this reality of creation as a living and dynamic relationship alive with the beauty and goodness of God. The Otoe-Pawnee teacher and writer Anna Lee Walters describes this spiritual tradition of her people in her book, *Talking Indian: Reflections on Survival and Writing.*

"*Waconda* in the Otoe language is known as the *Great Mystery*, that vital thing or phenomenon in life that cannot ever be entirely comprehensible to us. What is understood though, through the spoken word, is that silence is also *Waconda*, as is the universe and everything that exists, tangible and intangible, because none of these things are separate from the life force. It is all *Waconda*."

Native American spirituality views nature as something we live within, which calls us to reverence, respect, and humility. Mother Earth is divine. Water, animals, places, trees, and even stones possess spirits that interact with us in a way of spiritual harmony. For example, the cherry tree symbolizes rebirth and compassion and has healing properties helping with digestion. The elm is important in gaining wisdom and strength of will and provides a salve for wounds.

Animals are also perceived as sacred and act as spirit guides, coming to us in times of need. The bear is a sign of spiritual and physical power and courage. The bear claw, often worn by those who seek leadership, represents protection. The butterfly is seen as an image of transformation, a communicator in dreams, and a symbol of peace. The crow represents the mystery of creation, intelligence, perspective, and fearlessness. The falcon signifies vision, knowledge, and decisiveness. The circle is an important sacred symbol for Native Americans and represents the sun, the moon, the cycles of the seasons, and the cycle of life to death to rebirth. Native Americans pray and dance in a circle to honor the Creator.

> *Love settles within the circle, embracing it and*
> *thereby lasting forever, turning within itself.*
> —Luther Standing Bear, Oglala Sioux

This spirituality is filled with wonderful folklore and oral tradition. These people share their customs, history, rituals, and legends through vivid tales. Here is an example of one of their most beautiful legends, from the book *American Indians Myths and Legends,* by Richard Erdoes and Alfonso Ortiz. It describes the creation of one of earth's loveliest creatures:

> One day the Creator was resting, sitting, watching some children at play in a village. The children laughed and sang, yet as he watched them, the Creator's heart was sad. He was thinking: "These children will grow old. Their skin will become wrinkled. Their hair will turn gray. And those wonderful flowers, yellow and blue, red, and purple, will fade. The leaves from the trees will fall and dry up. Already they are turning yellow." Thus, the Creator grew sadder and sadder. It was in the fall, and the thought of the coming winter, with its cold and lack of game and green things, made his heart heavy. Yet it was still warm, and the sun was shining. The Creator watched the play of sunlight and shadow on the ground, the yellow leaves being carried here and there by the wind. He saw the blueness of the sky, the whiteness of some cornmeal ground by the women. Suddenly he smiled. "All those colors, they ought to

be preserved. I'll make something to gladden my heart, something for these children to look at and enjoy." The Creator took out his bag and started gathering things: a spot of sunlight, a handful of blue from the sky, the whiteness of the cornmeal, the shadow of playing children, the blackness of a beautiful girl's hair, the yellow of the falling leaves, the green of the pine needles, the red, purple, and orange of the flowers around him. All these he put into his bag. As an afterthought, he put the songs of the birds in, too. Then he walked over to the grassy spot where the children were playing. "Children, little children, this is for you" and he gave them his bag. "Open it; there's something nice inside," he told them. The children opened the bag, and at once hundreds and hundreds of colored butterflies flew out, dancing around the children's heads, settling on their hair, fluttering up again to sip from this or that flower. And the children, enchanted, said that they had never seen anything so beautiful. The butterflies began to sing, and the children listened smiling. But then a songbird flying, settling on the Creator's shoulder, scolding him, saying: "It's not right to give our songs to these new, pretty things. You told us when you made us that every bird would have his own song. And now you've passed them all around. Isn't it enough that you gave your new playthings the colors of the rainbow?" "You're right," said the Creator. "'I made one song for each bird, and I shouldn't have taken what belongs to you." So, the Creator took the songs away from the butterflies, and that's why they are silent.

My great-great-grandmother was a member of the Micmac tribe. The Micmac are one of the North American Indian tribes traditionally occupying Nova Scotia, New Brunswick, and Prince Edward Island and parts of Maine and Massachusetts. Micmac is also spelled *Mi'kmaq*, which means "my friends" in their language. Although early reports from Jacques Cartier said the Micmac appear fierce and warlike, they were early to adopt Christian teachings from the French Jesuits. On June 24, 1610, Grand Chief Membertou converted to Catholicism and was baptized. St. Anne Mission on Chapel Island in Nova Scotia is a famous pilgrimage site for the Mi'kmaw people.

Here is one of their beautiful Mi'kmaq prayers: Creator, open our hearts to peace and healing between all people. Creator, open our hearts to provide and protect all children. Creator, open our hearts, to end exclusion, violence, and fear among all. Thank you for the gifts of this day.

Celtic Spirituality

Carl McColman, in his book, *An Invitation to Celtic Wisdom: A Little Guide to Mystery, Spirit, and Compassion* writes, "Celtic spirituality represents the wisdom of a people who never were conquered by the Roman Empire, so they preserved an ancient way of seeing and knowing that was lost elsewhere. Living as they did on the very end of the world, the Celts forged an identity anchored in a deep sense of nature, a love of their land, a passion for kinship, and a love for the Spirit that embraced beauty and silence, solitude and self-forgetfulness, deep peace and deep listening." Everyday life for the ancient Celts of Ireland, Wales, and Scotland, was spiritually significant, sacred, and meaningful. The beliefs and practices had roots in the wisdom of desert spirituality.

For the ancient Celts, life itself was an observance with rituals and time was Kairos blessed. Specific prayers accompanied all action from milking the cows in the morning to lighting and keeping the fire at night. Here is a wonderful example of one of their daily prayers which was certainly influenced by St. Patrick: "God to enfold me, God to surround me, God in my speaking, God in my thinking. God in my sleeping, God in my waking, God in my watching, God in my hoping. God in my life, God in my lips, God in my soul, God in my heart. God in my sufficing, God in my slumber, God in my ever-living soul, God in my eternity."[8]

Celtic life had monastic overtones since many monasteries were built in Ireland after its conversion by St. Patrick in the fifth century. God's grace, presence, and love pervaded

---

[8] Alexander Carmichael, *Carmina Gadelica: Hymns and Incantations* (Edinburgh: Floris Books, 1994), 83.

everything. Even matter was infused with divine presence and dreams, and thin places offered experiences of God and portals to a world beyond this one. Known for its storytelling, poetry, dance, music, and the arts, this spirituality, like the Native Americans, excels in oral tradition with rich imagination.

The Celts have their share of delightful legends as well. Ciaran of Clonmacnoise was known as one of the "Twelve Apostles of Ireland." Preaching primarily to the Irish pagans of his time, Ciaran went to a woodland to build himself a small hermitage. The early monks sought out remote places of silence and solitude, following the desires of their souls to hear the voice of God. Many of these became known as edge places and thresholds, where heaven and earth came together.

Resting by a tree, he noticed a ferocious boar approaching. He spoke gently to him, calling him "Brother Boar." The boar stopped in his tracks. He befriended him and began to help Ciaran to build his hermitage by tearing down strong branches with his teeth and laying them at his feet. When the small place was finished, the boar remained with Ciaran. Not long after, other animals began to join them, including a wolf, a fox, a badger, deer, and assorted birds. Ciaran referred to them as his first brother monks.

Ciaran later built a monastery on the site, and Clonmacnoise became one of the largest and the most-significant centers of learning in Ireland. Ciaran's remarkable stories with his animals continued, with his fox carrying his Psalter back and forth to him so he could pray. The monastery's milking cow was so revered that when she died, her hide became a kind of relic and was said to offer healing. And Ciaran himself used the antlers of a live stag as a kind of book rest at his time for study. St. Ciaran, known as "a light of shining knowledge," died of a plague at the age of thirty-three, within a year after the monastery of Clonmacnoise was built.

Other ancient folklore has stories of Celtic missionaries leaving their monasteries to spread the gospel, starting out on seafaring voyages, *rudderless,* trusting God would lead them safely and directly to their missions. Called holy wanderings, or *Peregrinatio pro Christo,* (adventures with Christ*),* these missionaries entered boats, called coracles, letting the winds and tides bring them to their evangelical destinations, where they remained until they died. Before setting out, these courageous men "wandering for the love of Christ," often prayed a Celtic "Caim," an encircling prayer such as this one: "The God of the elements' guarding, the loving Christ's guarding, the Holy Spirit's guarding, be cherishing me, be aiding me."

One legend has it that Columba and Adamnan, the abbots of Iona, experienced this form of prayer. St. Adamnan said that when St. Columba sailed from Loch Foyle, he blessed a stone by the water's edge and made a circle round it sunwise. From that stone, he went into the boat. St. Columba instructed that anybody going on a journey who did this prayer round the stone would most likely arrive in safety.

The *Caim* is a place of sanctuary, an invisible circle of protection. To pray a *Caim,* you begin the invocation with an arm extended outward and your pointer finger set toward the ground, tracing the shape of a circle. This creates a sacred circular space around you in which you invoke the protection of God. You do not need to limit it to yourself. You can extend that circle in your prayerful imagination to include your loved ones, your home, and the world. Here is a beautiful *Caim* often prayed at Celtic weddings and family celebrations: "Circle us, Lord. Keep love within, keep hatred out. Keep joy within, keep fear out. Keep peace within, keep worry out. Keep light within, keep darkness out. May you stand in the circle with us, today and always."

Both Native American and Celtic spiritualities reveal crossing borders of soulful longing, timelessness, and passageways. They lived their daily lives with spirit-filled experiences of faith and trust in the reality of a presence existing in all the circles of life.

Theophanies

The Word is living, being, spirit, all
verdant greening, all creativity.
This Word manifests itself in every creature.
—Hildegard of Bingen

During the Middle Ages, nature was called the "little word" of God. This was not just because God spoke and the world came into being, but also because nature itself announces to us a *theophany* of God. *Theophany* is a Greek word, meaning "appearance of God." The Irish theologian John Scotus Eriugena, in the ninth century, taught that there are two books of revelation: the book of Holy Scriptures and the book of creation. Both are needed for us to know the divine presence.

This concept of the book of creation is one in which the essence of God, as that of light, life, and love, reveals all nature as holy. All God's creatures, plant life, and landscapes are sacred. Holy. My Ned was sacred—a special manifestation of God's love, peace, and consolation.

Norman Wirzba, a professor of theology at Duke University, has written in his book *From Nature to Creation*: "For Christians the world is creation, and to know what creation means we have to look to Jesus and to the history of God's revelation, which finds its climax in him. If this is true, that means that when Christians look carefully at the world, when they peer beyond the surface of things, what they should see is Jesus and his love moving through everything."

Have you ever experienced a theophany? A time in which God's presence infused a place, event, or person? Were you seeking it, or did the experience *come upon you* surprisingly?

You may want to take a little time now and journal these remembrances as "Theophanies of My Life."

Have you ever had the experience of an intense feeling of peace, love, or strength flow through you?

Have you ever been out in nature and noticed a particular flower, plant, tree, weed, cloud, or stone and felt close to it? Did you want to take it home with you? Describe that experience.

Write about a mysterious encounter or a special affinity with an animal, wild or domestic, where you felt heart-to heart communication. Describe this.

Have you ever had a moment, gazing out on a rainstorm, absorbed in a wind or breeze, enjoying a time spent in water, the ocean, or a lake, lying on a beach, in grass, or under the sun, when you felt time stopped and you were one with nature?

TWELVE
The Learner

BECOMING A NEW CREATION

So whoever is in Christ is a new creation;
the old things have passed away;
behold, new things have come.
—2 Corinthians 5:17

A s time moved on, in the midst of praying my vocation prayer, I asked Jesus to help me know and love Him. As I meditated on the New Testament and read various visionary writings, I became more familiar with the loving words and actions of Jesus and my devotion for Him grew. I also learned more about the Apostles and the various characters of the Gospels. Mary Magdalene especially intrigued me. So much so, I prayed to her and requested that she be a guide in my vocation. Her courage, tenacity and undaunting love for Jesus attracted me and I wanted to model myself after her. Leaving her past behind, she intrepidly followed Jesus into an unknown future. Steadfastly, and full of hope and trust, she re-created herself through the grace of God.

This "Apostle to the Apostles" is conceivably, after the Virgin Mary, the most celebrated woman of the Gospels. Pope

Francis elevated the memorial of Mary Magdalene to the status of Feast on July 22nd, 2016 in order to stress the importance of this faithful disciple of Christ who was the first to proclaim the Resurrection.

I later learned that she is a saint beloved by Carmelites. St. Teresa of Avila, St. Therese, and St. Elizabeth of the Trinity, to name a few, were inspired by her daring and loyal dedication to Jesus, as she bravely witnessed His death on the Cross, earnestly sought Him at the tomb, and lovingly adored Him, newly risen from the dead.

Holy Wanderings

Faith and hope are theological virtues that work together to bring us to love, the third and greatest theological virtue that will follow us into eternal life. Having faith and hope that our desires and prayer requests are heard and answered by God and the saints is a taste of eternity now. It reveals the creation story as an ongoing process in which we all participate and have a role to play—sometimes a "new" role.

One beautiful, autumn Saturday afternoon, I went driving west of Boston on an impromptu foliage trip. At the time, I did not know I was actually taking part in a kind of *holy wandering* experience. I ended up at the Divine Mercy Shrine in Stockbridge, Massachusetts. I was thirty-four years old. Because I was new to the place, I was slowly driving up to the huge shrine to park, and I saw a sister walking. For some reason, I felt the need to talk to her. I put the window down, pulled alongside her, and asked if I could speak to her. She shook her head and whispered, "I am on a retreat."

I said, "Oh! I am so sorry I interrupted your prayer."

Then she looked at me again, smiled, pointed to a building, and said, "Follow me." She brought me to a retreat house, took me to a visiting room, and we spoke for about two hours. I immediately felt comfortable opening up to her, and I related all I had been experiencing and how my desires were growing. She was the first person to tell me I had a vocation to a religious life. Her name was Sr. Mary Magdalene.

About seven months later, I visited the Poor Clares in Jamaica Plain, a neighborhood in Boston. I had noticed the monastery when I had walked the Arnold Arboretum, a two-hundred-plus acre botanical garden with trees from around the world. The monastery adjoins the garden. I did not make an appointment; I just showed up after a walk and asked to speak to the vocation director. She met with me for about an hour, affirmed me in my vocation, and wanted me to come back to discern. Her name was Sr. Mary Magdalen.

Now, looking back, I realized that many of my holy wanderings had commonalities:

- I was alone.
- I was gazing at nature—specifically, trees, sky, and clouds.
- I was relaxed.
- There were no time constraints.
- There was incredible beauty to behold.
- It was all-new and soul-stirring.
- I was aware of opening horizons, a becoming.
- Everything happened peacefully.
- There was a need in me to move and to experience something.
- There was a surprise waiting for me to find in my adventures.

Even at the Kellogg School of Management, when I was somewhat tired, the night was just too spectacular to stay in and study after dinner. I felt compelled to go out and experience the beauty of the campus. Subsequently, I found the book *The Practice of the Presence of God*. Nature itself, as creation, was assisting my soul with the transformation in which my body was unconsciously participating. God speaks to us in beauty. The Spirit is present in every moment; we need the eyes to see and ears to hear. My soul, operating within the beauty of nature and Kairos time, was beginning to move my body more powerfully into action and the discernment of a new life—a future filled with hope.

In that wonderful book, *From Nature to Creation*, Norman Wirzba detailed these changes taking place: "Creation, we might say, flows from Jesus at its beginning, flows through Jesus as it is healed, and flows to Jesus as it is fulfilled. Jesus is the pivot of the universe's movement and the key to its deep meaning and significance ... Just as Jesus redefined the world, he was also re-creating humanity so that each person could live in a way that contributed to creation's flourishing. As the apostle Paul put it succinctly in his second letter to the Corinthians, "Insofar as people are 'in Christ' they are no longer themselves: they are a 'new creation' (2 Corinthians 5:17), and part of a world in which the old is passing away and everything is becoming new."

PART III

The Life of Living Love

THIRTEEN
The Server

THE MEANING OF LIFE

Joy is the emotional expression of the
courageous YES to one's own true being.
Paul Tillich, *The Courage to Be*

Paul Tillich, one of the most influential philosophers and theologians of the twentieth century, wrote in his book *The New Being*: "Christianity is the message of the New Creation, the New Being, the New Reality ... We belong to the Old Creation, and the demand made upon us by Christianity is that we also participate in the New Creation."

All of creation is God's revelation in the process. God's grace in action. God's will unfolding. In the book of Revelation, God, who is seated on His throne states "Behold, I am making all things new" (Revelation 21:5). We are meant to be part of this glorious new creation and new reality. Here and now.

According to Tillich, "Where the New Reality appears, one feels united with God, the ground and meaning of one's existence. One has what has been called the love of one's destiny. One accepts oneself as something which is eternally important, eternally loved, eternally accepted. There is a center ... a meaning for life."

A lack of meaning in our lives has been associated with alcohol abuse and drug addiction or mental health problems such as anxiety and depression. Sadness and lethargy are all characteristics of people working toward goals or in relationships that tend to conflict with their senses of inner self. Their souls. The result is a sense of a "miss" or hopelessness, feelings of aimlessness, emptiness, and apathy—or worse, burnout.

The Maslach Burnout Inventory was created by Christine Maslach, a professor at University of California, Berkeley. Burnout characteristics are as follows: a diminished sense of self-efficacy or personal accomplishment, emotional exhaustion, and depersonalization. Maslach elaborates further to define burnout as "an erosion of the soul caused by a deterioration of one's values, dignity, spirit, and will."

Obviously, this soul erosion impacts not only a work-life, but also the entire life. Having a sense of purpose, loving, caring for others, or feeling that one is making the world a better place are all key factors in countering the effects of burnout. One method of healing is called logotherapy. Logotherapy was developed by neurologist and psychiatrist Viktor Frankl, who was convinced that if we search primarily for happiness, we will not find it. Rather, human beings are to search for *meaningfulness*, and from this, happiness, hope, and self-worth comes.

Frankl's ideas are summarized by these three points:

- Our primary motivation is our will to find meaning in life.
- Meaning can be found in any circumstances when we give ourselves over to something greater than ourselves, whether that is a cause or another person.
- We always have the freedom to find meaning, even in the face of unchangeable suffering.

Frankl's views were based on his real-world experiences at the Nazi concentration camp Auschwitz, in 1944. After miraculously surviving his prison experience, he went on to write his famous book *Man's Search for Meaning.* This book has sold over ten million copies and been translated into twenty-four languages. I have adjusted his quote with inclusive language: "The more one forgets oneself—by giving oneself to a cause to serve or another person to love—the more human one is and the more one actualizes oneself. What is called self-actualization is not an attainable aim at all, for the simple reason that the more one would strive for it, the more they would miss it. In other words, self-actualization is possible only as a side-effect of self-transcendence."

Self-transcendence, from a theological perspective, is the action of the divine life within the human person. It originates through a personal relationship with God, who is truth and love. We cannot self-transcend ourselves. The experience of self-transcendence results not from the ego's effort to fulfill its every desire, but from a movement beyond that self-centeredness in an attempt to work toward the good of others. It is the soul in action. Charity in action.

This involves the gifts and the fruits of the Holy Spirit being activated to bring forth the kingdom of God in us and, ultimately, through us. Only in this way will we find true fulfillment in our lives. It is a joy of giving that is offered. But how do we find the best way to give ourselves away? How do we discern our callings or vocations? How do we discover what the call to serve means for us?

To Serve with Love

*The best way to find ourselves is to lose
ourselves in the service of others.*
—Shawn Askinosie

Shawn Askinosie was a top criminal defense lawyer representing cases involving the death penalty or life imprisonment. He received multiple death threats as he won his cases. Consistently. In an article in *Forbes* magazine he relates, "The stakes were very high. I loved it. It was my calling at the time." Until it wasn't. After more than twenty years, his body began to send him messages that he shouldn't be doing this anymore. At one point in the midst of one of his last court cases, he was hospitalized with symptoms of a heart attack that turned out to be a panic attack. This event initiated a five-year new-job search that began each day with this prayer: "Please, God, give me something else to do."

This journey from being an attorney to becoming a chocolatier was so compelling and inspiring that he felt the need to share his experience. So, in 2017, he and his daughter, Lauren, the company's chief marketing officer, wrote the book *Meaningful Work: A Quest to Do Great Business, Find Your Calling, and Feed Your Soul. Forbes* recently named his family business, Askinosie Chocolates, as one of the top twenty-five small companies in America.

Their mission is to serve their farmers, (the cocoa farmers from Tanzania and the Philippines, share in 10 percent of the profits), their neighborhood, their customers, and each other, sharing the Askinosie experience by leaving the world a better place than they found it. The company, to date, has provided over a million school lunches to malnourished children in Tanzania and the Philippines and is regarded as a vanguard in the industry.

Shawn became a Family Brother at Assumption Abbey, a Trappist monastery near Ava, Missouri, and is cofounder of Lost and Found, a grief center serving children and families in Southwest Missouri. His father, a former lawyer, died in his arms of lung cancer at Assumption Abbey, when Shawn was fourteen years old. That unresolved grief and sorrow resurfaced during his job search and powerfully impacted his amazing vocation journey. Dealing with—and subsequently healing—that broken heartedness opened the path of new meaning and joy in his life. He explains, "It's really, really hard for people to find their passion, and to translate that into what they do in their daily lives is just massively complex."

Shawn developed steps within his book to assist in finding your own vocation. His basic premise is that when you lose yourself to serving someone or something, you find your truest self (your soul) and discover meaning in your life in the process. He recommends taking the time to be alone, ponder, and pray to rediscover your passions, talents, and skills, and to make use of them in new and vital ways of service that will change your world and the worlds of those you serve.

The true spiritual path to your vocation is one of action, which takes courage. You need to "go it alone." The path is yours; no one can make this journey for you. And your soul knows where to go.

FOURTEEN
The Server

RE-CREATING OUR LIVES

For we are His handiwork, created
in Christ Jesus for good works
that God prepared in advance,
that we should live in them.
—Ephesians2:10

We can take small steps to re-create our lives by daily acts of charity. It takes courage and determination to make bigger, life-changing steps, but love shows the way. He *is* the way.

It was late on an Easter Sunday night when I realized it was time for me to quit Polaroid and discern my religious vocation full time. I was thirty-six, and it was one year after my dad's death. For the three previous years, I had been gradually changing my life. I had been going to daily Mass and monthly confession, volunteering in various places, and was spiritually reading, studying, and praying. That Sunday, after Easter dinner, my mother gave me a book by Saint Teresa of Calcutta called *A Simple Path*. My mom had received it as a gift and thought I would like it. Mother Teresa's goal in the book was to inspire her readers to move from spiritual practices to lives of action and loving service. I finished it around midnight that same night. The last sentence was Matthew 25:40, which said, "Whatsoever you did to the least of my brothers and sisters, you did for me."

I felt moved to pray, and I said, "Lord, if this is what I think it is, I need another sign." So, I picked up *My Daily Bread*, knelt down, and opened it at random and read, "Whatsoever you did to the least of my brothers, you did for me" (Matthew 25:40).

I didn't sleep all night. I pondered how I would resign from Polaroid and tell my family and friends about this decision. I knew they would be shocked. I did not want to say I was considering religious life at that time. So, I left the resignation reason as a need for a kind of sabbatical. I wanted to explore the field of human services, particularly investigating working with troubled youth, which was true. I had long thought of taking time off and volunteering at Covenant House in New York City, which assists teen runaways. Financially, I was fine, so this exploration could last for a few years.

I resigned the next day, Easter Monday, and gave the company two weeks. It was mid-April. The second quarter marketing and sales plans were in full swing and products were in place. It was the perfect time to go. After leaving, I remember that spring—May, in particular—as being especially beautiful. I enjoyed every minute of it!

Nepsis Life

In the beginning was the Word, and the Word
was with God, and the Word was God.
All things came to be through him, and
without him nothing came to be.
What came to be through him was life . . .
—St. John 1:1–3

When we act from our souls, our bodies begin the means of transfiguration, changing into a more spiritual state of awareness and watchfulness. The Orthodox call this *nepsis*. Our sight becomes sharper, more intuitive. Our hearing holds more understanding. We *feel* more. Compassion is stronger in our judgements and actions. Synchronicity experiences are recognized and begin to propel us into our future. In logotherapy, every moment holds meaning and cues for our lives. It is an awareness of becoming potentiality God's will in action. These changes, over time, are imperceivable but real. A philosophical way to look at this is that the Word (in Greek, the *Logos)*, becomes active in us.

God is the master architect of the Kingdom of God. We all have an important role to play in this plan. Each of us have our own blueprints, called *logoi*. All *logoi* are united and act *within* the *Logos's* divine nature and creative energy. We are all one in Christ, who is the Word of God. The *Logos*. The second person of the Trinity. *Logoi* is "act" and "potential" within us. It is a dormant seed planted, awaiting the conditions beneficial to its growth that will transform our lives and offer a very different experience of who we are. This transformation is so significant that it is said to be like awakening from sleep or being reborn into a new life.

In his book, *Et Introibo Ad Altare Dei* (I Will Go unto the Altar of the Lord), Orthodox Archbishop Alexander Golitzin explains, "The *logoi* are our personal and foreordained vocations to which we may or may not choose to become conformed—or better—since they remain transcendent by virtue of their source in God—to which we may choose to be ever in process of becoming conformed in order thus to share, as it were, in the eternal process of our own creation."

As we choose to conform our wills to the "thought wills," the *logoi* of God, we echo and mirror God's preexisting idea for our lives. We find our lives' meaning in fulfilment of our individual *logoi* energy, which is united in God. We *become* what we were meant to be.

After the fall in the garden of Eden, we lost the wisdom and ability to act in union with the *Logos*. This form of spiritual awareness is named *natural contemplation,* or *theoria physike,* by the masters of long ago. According to Maximus the Confessor, an Orthodox monk, theologian, and mystic of the seventh century, the *Edenic* consciousness was taken from us by original sin. However, those who regain their "purity in heart" recover this knowledge and perceive this hidden wisdom in nature and in themselves. Acting as cocreators, they recognize and fulfill God's will and plan for creation through the work of their hands and minds. This is grace in action. Love in action. The Spirit in action. The soul in action.

A Living Blueprint

It is very dangerous to go into eternity with
possibilities which one has oneself prevented
from becoming realities. A possibility is a
hint from God. One must follow it.
—Søren Kierkegaard

When studying the philosophical concepts of "Logos and logoi" and "being and becoming," one can go to the masters of the past, Plato, Maximus the Confessor, Augustine, Thomas Aquinas, or Don Scotus—or one can go to metaphysicians of recent times like Martin Heidegger, Jacques Maritain, and Dietrich von Hildebrand. Or even to the very recent John McTaggart. I went to one of my favorite Carmelite sisters, Edith Stein, known in Carmel as St. Teresa Benedicta of the Cross.

Born in 1891 to a Jewish family in Germany, Edith, an outstanding student, became an atheist in her teenage years. The "search for truth" marked her entire spiritual journey. This concluded in her understanding, years later, that "all who seek truth, seek God, whether this is clear to them or not." A brilliant philosopher, she wrote her doctoral dissertation, as did Dietrich von Hildebrand, under the direction of Edmund Husserl, the founder of phenomenology. She later became his teaching assistant. Phenomenology, in simple terms, is the philosophic study of self-awareness and the development of human consciousness.

One evening, as a summer guest in a fellow doctoral student's home, Edith, then thirty-one years old, took a book from their library, *The Autobiography of St. Teresa of Avila*, to read for the night. She could not put it down and had finished it by morning. "When I had finished the book, I said to myself: This is truth." Later, looking back on her life, she wrote: "My longing for truth was a single prayer." After this profound conversion, she was baptized into the Catholic Church. A prolific German writer, researcher, teacher, and lecturer for the next eleven years, Edith experienced a call to Carmel and entered the Carmelite Monastery of Cologne, in 1933, at age forty-two. A year later, she received the habit and became Sr. Teresa Benedicta of the Cross.

In the Carmelite monastery, she was encouraged to keep writing and wrote the book *Finite and Eternal Being*, among others, which is considered her masterpiece. It was unpublished at the time of her death in 1942, when she died in the concentration camp at Auschwitz.

In him [Christ] we also have obtained an inheritance,
having been predestined according to the purpose of him
who works all things in accordance with the plan.

—Ephesians 1:11

In her book *Finite and Eternal Being*, St. Teresa Benedicta writes, "Every meaningful request (God makes) upon the soul is a word of God. For there is no meaning that does not have its eternal home and abode in the *Logos*. And anyone who willingly receives such a word of God simultaneously receives the divine power to comply with the demand." We must pray to allow our souls to lead us to recognize the divine Spirit, the divine life, and the divine love—or, as St. Teresa Benedicta says, "God Himself," who leads us to transformation. To transcendence. There is no randomness within our lives, for every moment is filled with His presence, His guidance, and His love.

St. Teresa Benedicta writes, "And the more lively becomes

the conviction of my faith that—from God's point of view—nothing is *accidental,* my entire life, even the minute-to-minute details, was predesigned in the plans of divine providence and is thus for the all-seeing eye of God a perfect coherence of meaning." The *logoi* is a living blueprint in the depths of our souls. It is the divinely designed imprint for our life's journey. This plan is filled with love and conforms us to our greatest good and happiness. Made in the "image of God" for the kingdom of God, we respond to and build upon this plan by following the will of God. The choice lies within us. However, our souls know the plan.

Initially, prayer, intention, and desire are the means and the way. St. Augustine said, "We move spiritually, not by our feet but by our desires." As we grow and we become more aware of the presence of God, the impulses of love will naturally reveal the way and the right thing to do. It will just "feel right." Jesus taught us a simple-yet-powerful prayer to lead us in fulfilling our roles in the kingdom of God. As we daily pray the "Our Father," may these words, "Your kingdom come, your will be done" (Matthew 6:10) echo a deeper meaning, reality, and fulfillment in our lives.

FIFTEEN
The Server

THE GROWING SOUL

I am yours; I was born for you.
What is your will for me?
—St. Teresa of Jesus (Avila)

In two of his poems, T. S. Eliot writes, "Humankind cannot bear very much reality" and "the heavy burden of the growing soul." What is the *growing soul*? It is the soul that leads. Cracks open our hearts to set out, offer, and serve. This reorienting is done invisibly, intrepidly, and imperceptivity. However, these changes can be daunting. Walking toward a new frontier can be overwhelming. But the soul steadily re-creates our new and expanded reality through the will of God.

What is reality? That is a *huge* metaphysical question for our culture today. The word *reality* has its root in *real*. What is real? What is true? What is truth? Or better yet, *who* is truth? The word *reality* was created by William James in 1985. James was a renowned American philosopher and was called the father of American psychology. His friends included Ralph Waldo Emerson, Bertrand Russell, Mark Twain, and Sigmund Freud.

My favorite quote of his is this: "We are like islands in the sea, separate on the surface but connected in the deep." So, what is reality? It is the totality of all things possessing actuality, existence, or essence. God is our *ever-present* reality—for "in Him, we live and move and have our being" (Acts 17:28). Rather than live our lives in the present moment, securely, as it unfolds before us, we seek to simulate our experiences. Construct and control our now. We have even created a "virtual reality."

As we age and experience the passing changes of time, we may be living our daily experiences mindlessly and very often be missing opportunities for change or symbols and cues for greater meanings for our existence, not "real-izing" the wisdom of and prospects for God's love and plan. In *Thoughts in Solitude,* Thomas Merton prays with the yearning of his heart for direction and the fulfillment of God's will in his life. It is a prayer we can all relate to as we strive to be open to our inscrutable futures and God's plan.

> My Lord, God, I have no idea where I am going. I do not see the road ahead of me. I cannot know for certain where it will end. Nor do I really know myself, and the fact that I think I may be following Your will does not mean that I am actually doing so. But I believe that the desire to please You does in fact please You. And I hope that I have that desire in all I am doing. I hope that I will never do anything apart from that desire. And I know that if I do this You will lead me by the right road, though I may know nothing about it. Therefore, I will trust You always though I may seem lost and in the shadow of death. I will not fear, for You are ever with me, and You will never leave me to face my perils alone.

The Sacraments of Time

Each incident, each event, each
suffering, as well as each joy
is a sacrament which gives God to (the soul).
—St. Elizabeth of the Trinity-Carmelite

Every moment holds God's presence, God's plan, and God's call to action. But what does God's call to action feel like? How do we perceive it? How do we serve? God acts in the here and now. The present moment. God is *living reality.* The great "I Am Who I Am" (Exodus 3:14). God seeks to act with us and through us. We are *called* to participate in the ongoing action and energy of God. So, when opportunity comes to us, if we are awake and watchful, our souls prompt our bodies to act and respond with love.

This beautiful, true story is in Kent Nerburn's book, *Make Me an Instrument of Your Peace: Living in the Spirit of the Prayer of St. Francis.*[9] He reveals, "The story is real, my friends. It was a gift of a moment to me, and I hope that by passing it along it is a gift to you, as well." Kent asked that I include the *whole* story in this book.

> "There was a time in my life twenty years ago when I was driving cab for a living. It was a cowboy's life, a gamblers life, a life for someone who wanted no boss, constant movement, and the thrill of a dice roll every time a new passenger got into the cab. What I didn't count on when I took the job was that it was also a ministry. Because I drove the night shift, the car

---

[9] Kent Nerburn, *Make Me an Instrument of Your Peace: Living in the Spirit of the Prayer of St. Francis* (San Francisco: HarperOne, 1999), 57–64.

became a rolling confessional. Passengers would climb in, sit behind me in total darkness and anonymity, and tell me of their lives. We were like strangers on a train, the passengers and I, hurtling through the night, revealing intimacies we would never have dreamed of sharing during the brighter light of day.

In those hours, I encountered people whose lives amazed me, ennobled me, made me laugh, and made me weep. And none of those lives touched me more than that of a woman I picked up late on a warm August night.

I was responding to a call from a small brick fourplex in a quiet part of town. I assumed I was being sent to pick up some partyers or someone who had just had a fight with a lover or someone going off to an early shift at some factory in the industrial part of town.

When I arrived at the address, the budding was dark except for a single light in a ground-floor window. Under these circumstances many drivers would just honk once or twice, wait a short minute, then drive away. Too many bad possibilities awaited a driver who went up to a darkened building at two-thirty in the morning.

But I had seen too many people trapped in a life of poverty who depended on the cab as their only means of transportation. Unless a situation had a real whiff of danger, I always went to the door to try to find the passenger. It might, I reasoned, be someone who needed my assistance. Would I not want a driver to do the same if my mother or father had called for a cab?

So, I walked to the door and knocked.

"Just a minute," answered a frail and elderly voice. I could hear the sound of something being dragged across the floor.

After a long pause, the door opened. A small woman, somewhere in her eighties, stood before me. She was wearing a print dress and a pillbox hat with a veil pinned on it, like you might see in a costume shop or a Goodwill store or in a 1940s movie. By her side was a small nylon suitcase. The sound had been her dragging it across the floor.

The apartment looked as if no one had lived in it for years. All the furniture was covered with sheets. There were no clocks on the walls, no knickknacks or utensils on the counters. In the corner was a cardboard box filled with photos and glassware.

"Would you carry my bag out to the car?" she said. "I'd like a few moments alone. Then, if you could come back and help me? I'm not very strong."

I took the suitcase to the cab, then returned to assist the woman. She took my arm, and we walked slowly toward the curb. She kept thanking me for my kindness. "It's nothing," I told her. "I just try to treat my passengers the way I would want my mother treated."

"Oh, you're such a good boy," she said. Her praise and appreciation were almost embarrassing. When we got into the cab, she gave me an address, then asked, "Could you drive through downtown?"

"It's not the shortest way," I answered.

"Oh, I don't mind," she said. "I'm in no hurry. I'm on my way to a hospice."

I looked in the rearview mirror. Her eyes were glistening. "I don't have any family left," she continued. "The doctor said I should go there. He says I don't have very long."

I quietly reached over and shut off the meter. "What route would you like me to go?" I asked.

For the next two hours we drove through the city. She showed me the building where she had once worked as an elevator operator. We drove through the neighborhood where she and her husband had lived when they had first been married. She made me pull up in front of a furniture warehouse that had once been a ballroom where she had gone dancing as a girl.

Sometimes she would have me slow down in front of a particular building or corner and would sit staring out into the darkness, saying nothing. As the first hint of sun was creasing the horizon, she suddenly said, "I'm tired. Let's go now."

We drove in silence to the address she had given me. It was a low building, like a small convalescent home, with a tar driveway that passed under a portico. Two orderlies came out to the cab as soon as we pulled up. Without waiting for me, they opened the door and began assisting the woman. They were solicitous, intent, watching her every move. They must have been expecting her; perhaps she had phoned them right before we left.

I opened the trunk and took the small suitcase up to the door. The woman was already seated in a wheelchair. "How much do I owe you?" she asked, reaching into her purse.

"Nothing," I said.

"You have to make a living," she answered.

"There are other passengers," I responded. Almost without thinking, I bent over and gave her a hug. She held on to me tightly.

"You gave an old woman a little moment of joy," she said. "Thank you."

There was nothing more to say. I squeezed her hand once, then walked out into the dim morning light. Behind me I could hear the door shut. It was the sound of the closing of a life.

I did not pick up any more passengers that shift. I drove aimlessly, lost in thought. For the remainder of that day, I could hardly talk. What if that woman had gotten a driver who had been angry or abusive or impatient to end his shift? What if I had refused to take the run or had honked once, then driven away? What if I had been in a foul mood and had refused to engage the woman in conversation? How many other moments like that had I missed or failed to grasp?

We are so conditioned to think that our lives revolve around great moments. But great moments often catch us unawares. When that woman hugged me and said that I had brought her a moment of joy, it was possible to believe that I had been placed on earth for the sole purpose of providing her with that last ride. I do not think that I have ever done anything in my life that was any more important."

The Divine Plan

*The realization that God is active in
all that happens at every moment
is the deepest knowledge that we can
have in this life of the things of God.*
—Jean-Pierre de Caussade

The Sacrament of the Present Moment is a slim volume spiritual classic by Jean-Pierre de Caussade, a French Jesuit and spiritual director in the eighteenth century. Originally titled *Self-Abandonment to Divine Providence*, this mystical treatise recounts that "time is but the history of divine action." Jean-Pierre writes, "Everything that happens to us, in us and through us, embraces and conceals God's divine but veiled purpose, so that we are always being taken by surprise and never recognize it until it has been accomplished." This is the secret of the spiritual life, to gracefully live by the hand of God. God's purposes and will, our security and happiness. This is Edenic consciousness. A living by our souls.

Thomas Merton in his wonderful book *Thoughts in Solitude* wrote, "If you want a spiritual life, you must unify your life. A life is either all spiritual or not all. No one can serve two masters. Your life is shaped by the end you live for. You are made in the image of what you desire." This unified life is one of contemplation, which is aware that all life transcends from an invisible source from which it has come and to which it will go back, fulfilling its purpose. This return to the Father, in Christ, is always beginning now, through our oneness with Christ. This union, which is a state of total self-surrender, meekness, and humility, allows the Holy Spirit to act in us only with our complete trust. This is what it means to be pure of heart, relying on God's providence for everything, moment by moment. Blessed are the pure of heart, for they will *see* God!

Paschal Mystery

A Redemptorist priest in a homily told of a novice director redefining the EGO in this way—"Easing God Out." Actually, evil starts here as it started in the garden, with the lie that we are our own masters and create our own futures. We manifest our own destinies. In a culture of individualism, the ego is king. The soul and conscience have been silenced. This mindset can then lead to sin or, in extremes, to despair, which is a lack of hope or meaning. To live by the hand of God does not mean we are free from suffering, pain, disappointment, tragedy, or failure. Moral evils, such as murder, human and drug trafficking, pedophilia, and natural evils such as earthquakes, viruses, cancer, are ongoing situations that involve piercing human suffering.

Our monastery receives calls and emails daily asking for prayers from people dealing at some level with addiction, mental illness, divorce, Alzheimer's, chemo and radiation treatments, unemployment, gang violence, and unwanted pregnancies. Every human life has a full experience of trials and temptations, fears and dreams, and joys and sorrows. But *living* faith and hope supports us in our everyday struggles during our pilgrimages here on earth.

St. Teresa Benedicta of the Cross died as a martyr in Auschwitz. St. Elizabeth of the Trinity died at twenty-six from Addison's disease. Both Carmelites accepted the crosses that had been prepared for them and subsequently offered their sufferings, in union with Jesus, for the redemption of the world, as other Christs. Our share in the Passion story helps bring our brothers and sisters home. The Paschal Mystery of Jesus is lived by each one of us who are part of the Mystical Body of Christ, whether we consciously *realize* it or not. We are not alone in our suffering and pain. Jesus is always with us.

SIXTEEN
The Leader

THE CALL OF THE SOUL

*Be who you were created to be
and set the world on fire.*
—St. Catherine of Siena

A vocation, or call, comes from God, and it is sacred. We were created to cocreate with God in His ongoing masterpiece, known as creation. This call may begin as a whisper and is often perceived as that. In our souls is an inherent need to creatively give of ourselves, our talents, and our time. Our vocations may have been found in childhood and become our occupations, such as doctors, nurses, or teachers, but not always. Some calls are experienced in the midst of a midlife crisis or severe trauma. Others come later, even in retirement.

In Richard Rohr's insightful book called *Falling Upward: A Spirituality for the Two Halves of Life,* he describes the first half of our lives' journeys as a seeking to establish our identities. We are set on ego achievement. Life is centered on *me.* As we age, we experience our failures, suffer from heartbreaks, and experience multiple life disappointments. Our rose-colored glasses begin to crack. This is *falling* upward. These are the necessary sufferings to learn lessons that paradoxically are the stepping-stones to our self-knowledge, self-acceptance, and self-surrender for the second half of our journeys, which is a *rising* to new life.

Richard Rohr explains, "Sooner or later, some event, person, death, idea, or relationship will enter your life that you simply cannot deal with … Spiritually speaking, you will be, you must be, led to the edge of your private resources. This is the only way that Life-Fate-God-Grace-Mystery can get you to change, let go of your egocentric preoccupations, and go on to the further and larger journey."

We "fall" through a particular life-altering situation only to suddenly rediscover our deeper and real lives, our true selves, or souls in God. This can lead to transformation and transcendence and to a newfound freedom and trustful surrender or to our giving back in gratitude and in service. There are no age guidelines for these stages; a ten-year-old dying of cancer may already be living in the second half of his or her life.

From a Carmelite perspective, this journey of symbolic dying and rising to new life has been named the "dark night of the soul," taken from a mystical poem by St. John of the Cross. The journey is called the dark night because darkness represents the hardships and difficulties we encounter in detaching from our ego prisons, or false selves, to living in peace and union from our true selves in God. Until we find ourselves in Him and *realize* His presence in the center of our souls, we are lost to the true significance of our lives.

In *The Silent Life*, a beautiful book of monastic meditation, Thomas Merton articulates "to live in Him is to live by His power, to reach from end to end of the universe in the might of His wisdom, to rule and form all things in and with Him. It is to be a hidden instrument of His Divine action, the minister of

His redemption, the channel of His mercy and the messenger of His infinite Love."

The Mystical Body of Christ is an image for the cosmic Christ who pervades and penetrates the entire universe. In this body of Christ, we are members and have an active and cocreative role to play. Our lives matter. Each role builds up the church, the world, the universe, and beyond.

Discovering Our Doors

Where your talents and the needs of the
world cross, therein lies your vocation.
These two, your talents and the needs of
the world, are the great wake-up calls to
your true vocation in life … to ignore this,
is in some sense, to lose your soul.
—Aristotle

If we are open to it, the lives we live are a never-ending journey of discovery. The giving of the self in all its ways transforms our lives and the lives of others. Some doors to new beginnings open even in the midst of our dark night experiences.

While walking alone on a beach, lost in her troubled thoughts, Lisa Honig Buksbaum distinctly heard a voice whisper the word, "Soaringwords." She did not understand what it meant, but there was no doubt in her mind that the voice was real. And it was a call to action. At the time, she was going through a very traumatic period of her life. Her thirty-five-year-old brother, her only sibling, had just died suddenly of an asthma-induced heart attack. Her dad was in the midst of his second bout of lymphoma, and her ten-year-old son was very sick with rheumatic fever.

Ten months later in 2001, with her father and son healed, Lisa acted on the voice. Closing her award-winning Manhattan marketing firm, Lisa founded a nonprofit organization helping critically ill and impoverished children and their families deal with life-threatening disease and treatments. She named her new venture, not surprisingly, Soaringwords. Lisa had experienced the joys of watching a seven-year-old as he spent days creating a rainbow unicorn for another sick child. After supporting a study, she found that those ill children who had been given the chance to make simple gifts for other sick children felt significantly better about themselves than those who weren't given the same opportunity. These creative children were more joyful, less worried, more excited, less tired, more hopeful, and less scared after doing something as simple as coloring a picture for another child.

Years later, Lisa understood that the word *soar* was an acronym. S.O.A.R. stands for Somatic response (relating to the body), Outcomes (actions that can be measured empirically), Agency (something that gives people a sense of control), and Reciprocity (the sense of being connected to others). Her global organization, now nineteen years old, provides fun, creative, and educational activities that enhance the lives of children, teens, and adults with well-being and healing.

Soaringwords has impacted more than five hundred thousand children in thirty states and twelve countries. She said, "As the Soaringwords lady, I am inspired by the quotation, 'What lies behind us and what lies ahead of us are simple matters compared to what lies within us.' Every day is an adventure and opportunity to transform ideas and collaborations into tangible things that inspire people to heal." This is second-half living done right. Done from her soul.

Understanding ourselves, our strengths, and our values is an important part of recognizing our natural abilities to serve. One of the most widely used psychological tests in the world is the Myers-Briggs Type Indicator. This introspective questionnaire was developed by Isabel Myers and her mother, Katherine Briggs, and was based on Carl Jung's theory of personality types. The test helps define what characteristics and motivations make you unique, how you perceive the world, and how you make decisions. The test results in four categories: introversion or extraversion, sensing or intuition, thinking or feeling, and judging or perceiving. One letter from each category is assigned to produce a four-letter test result, such as ENFP. There are sixteen personality types.

I found the test amazingly accurate. I am an INFJ. The careers best for this personality type are religious workers, psychologists, writers, web designers, artists, librarians, counselors, and teachers, to name a few. I found the personality traits included in the test results to be right on—both the good and the bad characteristics.

What is fascinating is that though these work inclinations were dormant in the first half of my life, they came on strong in my second half. I remember one of my freshman college professors, my favorite, told me to write, so I considered journalism, but the following year, I decided to pursue a business degree.

Currently, I am vocation director for our monastery and guide women in discernment and the first years of a religious vocation. I develop our websites, create podcasts on spirituality, manage our bookstore. This type of work never entered my mind growing up. I had to learn the technical skills to fulfill many of these obligations, so, when given—or asked to take on—this work, I took classes to gain confidence. I grew into these jobs, but they also came naturally to me.

Another test that provides wonderful insightful tools for understanding ourselves and others is the enneagram. This test has nine personality types. The philosophy behind the enneagram goes back to traditions from Judaism, Christianity, Islam, Taoism, Buddhism, and ancient Greek philosophy. After studying these wisdom traditions, Oscar Ichazo, a Bolivian, developed this test in the 1960s. Ichazo examined specifics about the structure of the human soul and about the ways in which the soul becomes distorted or contracted into states of ego. According to Ichazo's theory, there are nine main ways that we lose our centers and become distorted in our thinking, feeling, and doing. These nine passions, or ego-fixations, are the ways we forget our connections with God. However, there are also nine virtues corresponding to the passions that act as antidotes. We each have one primary ego-fixation and one primary virtue, and these are numbered. Knowing our "type" is a way to direct our inner selves in a spiritual transformative process so balance can be restored.

I encourage you to take these tests online and learn more about your natural abilities. Your strengths and your weaknesses. The inclinations that are inherent in you to help bring about the Kingdom of God.

The Graceful Giving

Deep within us is a need to live a life beyond success, a life of significance. To make a difference. Karl Rahner was one of the most brilliant and insightful theologians of the twentieth century. This Jesuit priest wrote volumes on Christology, Mysticism, and is known for *The Theology of Grace*. Rahner believed that everyone, even the agnostic or atheist, who lives in selfless service to others, lives what he calls the "mysticism of everyday life."

In *The Mystical Way in Everyday Life*, he writes,

> The simple and honestly accepted everyday life contains in itself the eternal and the silent mystery, which we call God and his secret grace ... To love God is first and foremost shown not by our ideals, our lofty words, our introspection, but by that act the rips selfishness away from us; by caring, through which we forget ourselves on account of another; by patience, which makes us silent and wise. People who place their small time into the heart of eternity which they already carry within, will suddenly realize that even small things have inexpressible depths, are messengers of eternity, and are always more than they appear to be ...

Grace is God's life in us. It is the authentic life of our souls and what our lives are truly called to be. Grace transforms our desires, motivations, and behaviors, and grounds and empowers everything in our lives. It is a subtle, but very real communication from God that is constant, though hidden.

St. Augustine and St. Thérèse of Lisieux had the view that "All is grace." Vocation involves recognizing and accepting God's ever-flowing grace. It is a total surrender to the unfolding reality of your life—a giving of your whole self into the hands of one who folded and created that reality for you *to* unfold. A moment-to-moment going forward into your future unfolding, pretty much blindfolded.

St. Teresa of Calcutta heard her *second call* whispered on a train and began as the *first m*issionary of charity by picking up one dying man on the streets of Calcutta and caring for him until he died in her arms. St. Paul makes it clear in his letter to the Corinthians that "God is able to make all grace abound to you, so that having all sufficiency in all things at all times, you may abound in every good work."

Pondering in Your Heart

One of the activities in chapter 7 of this book was to create a vision list. Now may be a good time to review the list you journaled. Or, if you did not do that exercise, it is a good time to begin. After reviewing your vision list did anything come as a surprise to you? What are your hopes? What are the ways you would like to spend your time? What is most important to you?

I encourage you now to answer the following questions, as applicable to you, and reflect on them deeply. Take your time, be honest, and write full paragraphs or multiple journal page answers.

- Do I look at our world in its poverty and pain? Do I seek to share in the anguish of a world in crisis? What problems really strike my heart and stir my soul?

- How important is my spiritual life to me? Are my faith and hope in God growing as I age? Do I see God's grace active in my life?

- What do I need more of? Less of?

- What do I see as the most pressing problem affecting our culture today? What am I most trying to protect myself and my loved ones from?

- What do I love to do? What makes me smile? Who makes me smile?

- How do my coworkers perceive me? How and when do I bring out the best in people?

- When am I at my best? When am I at my worst?

- Have I taken time to learn, ponder, and assist with improved changes regarding our environmental crisis? Am I considering the possible compromised future for the next generation? For my children and grandchildren?

- Am I a good parent? Have I nurtured my children with my time and energy? Have I fostered close and loving relationships to enhance their emotional, educational, and spiritual development? If I could teach them only one thing, what would it be?

- What inspires me?

- What would I like to create?

Now make three columns as follows and fill in the five spaces below with short bullet points.

My Soul's Desires   My Abilities   My Service & Helping

1.

2.

3.

4.

5.

How do you envision yourself best serving God and the needs of the world in your current life situation? What changes might be valuable to make?

SEVENTEEN
The Leader

NURTURING SOULS

Motherhood is a hallowed place because
children aren't commonplace. Co-laboring
over the sculpting of souls is a sacred vocation,
a humbling privilege. Never forget.
—Ann Voscamp, author of *One Thousand Gifts*

In the last chapter, you spent some quality time determining what legacy you would you want to leave to your children. Parenthood, nurturing souls that God has entrusted to you, I believe, is the number one leadership role in the world. Nothing is more important to the needs of the family, the society, and to our culture.

One of the most poignant times in my realization of parental importance took place in my close friend's kitchen many years ago. It was the celebration of the first newborn! Three of us had known each other since freshman year of high school and had—and have—remained very, very close. In fact, I am godmother to this *first mother's* third child.

We were in our midtwenties, and the baby was in a carrier on the kitchen table. Her father, another close friend, was with us. We were all gazing at this beautiful little person, and she was really beautiful! Really sweet. And really good. It was a like a miracle before our eyes. Actually, it was a miracle before our eyes. One of us said, "Wow! Amazing!" And then the dad said, "You know we just bought a new minivan with all the works, and it came with an instruction booklet that is about twenty-pages long. And the hospital just *gave* her to us, and we know nothing! It's kind of scary!" We all laughed, and so did the baby.

That family went on to have three more children of their own and then adopted three more, who were actually their biological nieces and a nephew. These adopted children, then aged six, three, and an infant, were rescued from a serious drug-addicted parental situation. All the kids are doing great; the youngest is in her senior year of high school. Needless to say, the parents have become experts in parenting. But it was not easy. The decisions to rescue, to get legally involved with, and later to adopt were a painful and emotional process for both families concerned.

Was it the right thing to do? Both sets of parents say absolutely. Was it in God's plan? It seems love showed the way, and grace was the driving force influencing all the changes, since the children were first found so neglected. My friend's first four children were all in school, and their family life had settled into a peaceful routine when the second family arrived so needy. Former family life for both would never be the same. All was radically changed for everyone. All seven personalities were affected as family rooms, dining rooms, bedrooms, and bathrooms were shared.

Did everyone heal? Yes. Was it very hard? Yes. Did it take a long time for the families to unite as one? Yes, years. Looking back, would they do it again? I don't know. I never asked my friend. But when I look at their Christmas card from three years ago, which has a full family photo, including a new son-in-law and additional sibling girlfriends and boyfriends smiling with their hands and arms interlocked at Thanksgiving, in Disney World, I would have to say, "Absolutely!"

Parents as Leaders

Don't worry that children never listen to you;
worry that they are always watching you.
—Robert Fulghum, author of *All I Really Need to*
Know I Learned in Kindergarten

In a survey of a thousand families, Ellen Galinsky, author of *Mind in the Making,* and head of the Family and Work Institute, asked children, "If you were granted one wish about your parents, what would it be?" The children's number one response was that their parents were less tired and less stressed.

Parenting is hard work, but it is often given the second or third place to what is done all day, which is the "real job." Ann Voscamp rightly called parenting—especially motherhood—a *sacred* vocation. The best parents have helping and supporting their children to grow into independent, loving and giving adults that contribute positively to society as their first goal and ongoing vocation. In his book *The Seven Habits of Highly Effective Families,* Steven Covey reveals his family's mission statement, which was constructed at a family meeting with all members contributing: "Mission Statement: The Mission of our family is to create a nurturing place of faith, order, truth, happiness, and relaxation and to provide opportunity for each individual to become responsibly independent, and effectively interdependent, in order to serve worthy purposes in society." Obviously, loving and helping each other is understood as the foundation of a strong and encouraging family dynamic.

It is in the family that children learn values, religious beliefs, and practices, respect for others, self-control, and meaning in life. Parents establish their own family cultures of what is right and wrong, and what is acceptable and not acceptable so that their children will go out into this world with a strong moral compass to guide them to become solid role models in a culture in need. It is in the family that religious faith and trust in God is learned. The first prayers. The first worship experiences.

Children naturally mirror their parents. I remember a neighbor telling me I had the same "walk" as my mom! It was sometimes difficult for people to tell my sister and my mom's voices apart on the phone. And those are just the tangible likenesses. Parents model authenticity, traits that children will carry their entire lives.

Parenting is formation, creating the foundational character for family generations to come. This translates into quiet courage in adversity or self-conscious anxiety, considerate respect for everyone or fearful racial prejudice, honest integrity or lying doubletalk. Parents are given the responsibility of forming lives of beauty that will become masterpieces of God's grace for our world or ill-formed lives of restlessness, sad dysfunction, and despair.

The Teaching Art

Creativity is as important as literacy.
—Sir Ken Robinson

The education system in the United States is being asked to do more with less: elementary and high school budgets are decreasing, principals are struggling to be instructional leaders in the face of enormous management issues, and teachers are trying to meet the needs of increasingly diverse students.

This situation has fostered a need to reimagine education and rethink how educators design schools, instruction, and who actually should be at the center of those changes. Sir Ken Robinson, former British author and educator, was known as one the world's elite thinkers on creativity and innovation. In his lifetime, he led multiple national and international projects on creative and cultural education across the world, seeking to unlock the creativity of students, teachers, and organizations. In February 2006, Sir Ken gave a TED Talk called "Do Schools Kill Creativity?'" This presentation has been viewed online over sixty-five million times and has been seen by an estimated 380 million people in 160 countries, making Sir Ken the most watched speaker in TED history.

In his talk, Sir Ken argued that the current educational systems are outdated, based on an industrial standardized paradigm, and that attending school has become more about finding the right answers to pass the tests than about creating stimulating divergent thinking. We are educating to produce good workers, rather than innovative, creative thinkers. Children, as natural learners, need to be taught to think critically and evaluate information.

It is essential that educators influence children's imaginations, cease from stigmatizing mistakes and do not stifle any forms of curiosity, for curiosity is the engine of learning. Sir Ken claimed, "The best evidence of human creativity is our trajectory through life. We create our own lives. And these powers of creativity, manifested in all the ways in which human beings operate, are at the very heart of what it is to be a human being."

We need to completely reimagine education.
—Fred Swaniker

Dr. Fred Swaniker is a Ghanaian entrepreneur and leadership development expert who has a passionate mission to establish better leadership in Africa and change his country into a leading economic force in the world. To this end, he has founded the African Leadership Academy, located outside Johannesburg in South Africa. The goal of the academy is to develop six thousand transformative leaders for Africa in a fifty-year time period. He is also the founder for the African Leadership University, a pan-African university offering programs to catalyze a new generation of three million ethical and entrepreneurial African leaders by 2060.

Dr. Swaniker wants to completely reimagine education so that students "learn how to learn" and how to solve problems instead of just facts and figures. This type of educating brings the working world into education a lot earlier and takes education earlier into the working world. "Education used to be a one-shot game, now it has to be a life-long game. You need to go in-between learning and work. You have to work on projects for real organizations from the beginning, and you have to go out into the environment, into communities. You have to understand the real problems that people are facing so you can shape your learning around those problems rather than just look at a textbook."

The students declare their life-missions and not a degree in their education. According to Dr. Swaniker, they pick a problem they want to solve and build their learning around that. "It is about giving a purpose to learning, and not just learning for learning's sake." This education creates leaders who are problem solvers, because as Dr. Swaniker attests, "Problem-solving will always be relevant even as the world changes."

America's Street Children

*They are like shadows in our cities, small
outlines of skin and bones that attach themselves
to abandoned buildings, park benches,
narrow alleyways. And when darkness falls,
these shadows disappear into places many
of us will never, ever see in this lifetime.*
—Sister Mary Rose McGeady, former president,
Covenant House

For more than four decades, Covenant House has helped transform and save the lives of more than a million homeless, runaway, and trafficked young people. They offer housing and support services to young people in need—currently reaching fifty thousand youth every year. Their work is guided by the mission statement to serve youth with absolute respect and unconditional love, to help kids who are suffering, and to protect and safeguard all children in need.

Covenant House does their mission well. I know. I volunteered in their faith community in Houston, Texas, for a year after leaving Polaroid. It was the most soul-stirring experience of my life. I found my vocation in the last months of my time serving in the organization. But back to the beginning.

My parents were Covenant House supporters, and they would receive books in the mail as part of their direct-mail campaigns. The stories about the runaways were unbelievable. They would easily make you cry. From early on, I wanted to volunteer and get involved. They were located in New York City at the time, and I was already working for Polaroid. At one point in my early thirties, I considered taking a sabbatical, but Polaroid did not approve it. The company countered with,

"How about getting your MBA? We will pay for that." After two months of boring night classes, in addition to full, exhausting days, that idea was shelved forever.

After I resigned in April, enjoying semiretirement for a few months, I called to investigate the faith community at Covenant House. I had never lived in community, had always had my own bedroom, and really did not know what "living in community" was all about. Investigating this new life was like entering into a new way of being with its own terminologies. I remember being interviewed and asked, "What are your gifts?"

I said, "My what?"

"Your God-given abilities. What can you do?"

I felt a little like an alien coming in from another planet. The Covenant House Faith Community staff approved me, and I started in New York the following January for a two-week training before my actual one-year faith-community assignment in February.

My group, from all over the country, varied in age from twenty-two to sixty-something, and half of them were discerning religious life. We learned the mission, had lunch with Sr. McGeady, and visited the New York City Covenant House location, shadowing workers for a few days. We provided three choices of potential assignment locations, and I was assigned to Houston.

Houston is one of the cleanest cities in the country. It is also home to the fastest and wildest drivers I've ever experienced. They are like cowboys on wheels. I am a native Bostonian driver, pretty fearless myself, but getting on and off the freeways of Houston, which is a huge and sprawling city, was like driving the Indianapolis 500. I did get used to it; you just ramp up and off at 75 mph.

The Kids

She didn't know what she was doing. She's sick.
—Jeremiah

My faith community had four members, two males and two females. We lived on the second floor of a very large house situated two blocks from Covenant House, Houston. Two of us were new, coming from New York, and the other two were in the last six months of their one-year assignment. They were all wonderful people, and I still keep in contact with a few of the community. At the time, everyone was seriously considering religious life, and within a few years, all were married and starting families.

My first six months were spent as a 3:00 p.m.–11:00 p.m. moms and babes staff-care member. This group supported unmarried young women with childcare while they went to GED class and work. We had full care of about ten to twelve children from infancy to six years old. In the last six months, I was a 3:00 p.m.–11:00 p.m. staff-care member for the minors, (age thirteen to seventeen) during the week, and for the eighteen to twenty-one-year-old group on the weekends.

The Catholic Women's League in Houston was incredible. It was composed of a wealthy group who supported Covenant House with donated tickets to *Cirque de Soleil*, the zoo, and to the museums and the planetarium. Every chance I got, I would take the minors offsite. They were my favorites, and their stories broke my heart.

Jeremiah had a hot iron marking on the inside of his left arm. His mother had pressed the iron directly into his skin and tried to hold it there. He told me she didn't know what she was doing. She was mentally ill. He had forgiven her, but he could not live with her anymore.

Harvey was thirteen when his grandfather dropped him at the front door. He said Harvey was uncontrollable and there was no way he could come home. Harvey never left my side for the last four months of my assignment. I checked in on him every night, shut off his light, and told him good night. He was fascinated at the planetarium, and at the gift store he saw stars and I bought them for his ceiling. No senior staff member ever curtailed me. They pretty much gave me free reign.

At *Cirque de Soleil*, Harvey sat next to me, and one of the four-year-olds that I had previously cared for was in front of us. Rihanna was known to be pretty wild. Her mom was pretty wild too. She saw me and wanted to sit on my lap. She and a few others used to "fix" or braid my hair as I sat on the floor in their midst while we watched *The Lion King* or *Aladdin* before bed. Halfway through the show, I got a cramp and Harvey said, "Miss Jeanne, I'll take her for you." He wrapped his arms around Rihanna, they both smiled, and at some point, she fell asleep. He carried her to the bus with me at the end of the show.

One night after dinner, the minor group and I had a God tree meditation. About ten of the children sat on couches in a circle, and we closed our eyes and I asked them to think of a huge tree, called the God tree. The tree was theirs and theirs alone. "Spend time with your tree," I said. "Envision it. What does it look like? Does it smell? What does it smell like? Where is located?"

We spent five minutes in meditation and then everyone was asked to share. Most said their trees were beautiful, and they sat underneath them and were happy. One fell asleep. One said she could not picture it at all. In a very quiet and sincere voice, Rick said that his tree was beautiful, but dogs were going to the bathroom all over it and he could not get them to stay away.

A few months before I began working with the minors and the eighteen- to twenty-one-year-olds, we were all at supper in the dining room, and I had responsibility for three children. Two were next to each other, in highchairs before me, and I had another seated on my right side. The other moms and babes staff had about seven more. So, the babe group was ten in all. We were all at the same large table. The minors were at their table, and there were a few eighteen- to twenty-one-year-olds at another table, although most of that group was at work.

Dinner was spaghetti, which everyone loved. I was helping to feed a baby girl, about eighteen months old, who was in one highchair, when the baby boy in the other highchair, who was about the same age, put his hand into his bowl, picked up some cut spaghetti, and threw it right into her face. I was shocked but tried not to laugh at her surprised, wide-eyed expression. Before I could say a thing, the baby girl picked up a fistful of her spaghetti and threw it right back into the baby boy's face. He looked at her in utter amazement, and they both started laughing gleefully. I could not help but laugh, and then the two of them did it again at the same time as I said, "No! Noooo!" Then our whole table of kids began to do it. A babe food fight was in full swing. When the two babies who had started everything realized they had no spaghetti left in their bowls, they started picking it off each other and eating it with joyful smiles.

The minors and the eighteen- to twenty-one-year-olds were laughing hysterically, watching the whole thing. Jeff, my faith community member who was the cook, was laughing too, but he kept looking at me as if to say, "Give me a break. I have to clean this whole thing up!" But he didn't. The minors and eighteen- to twenty-one-year-olds gladly helped him!

EIGHTEEN
The Leader

VOICES OF TRANSFORMATION

Our creative dreams and yearnings
come from a divine source.
As we move toward our dreams, we
move toward our divinity.
—Julia Cameron, *The Artist's Way: A Spiritual*
Path to Higher Creativity

Every age produces its artists, poets, sages, seers, saints, and visionaries. If they are people of integrity and passion, they inspire courage and influence change. Their works and lives reveal the transcendent values of beauty, truth, and goodness. Their expressions of creativity, such as the power of their music, or the beauty of their art or poetry come from the deepest parts of their souls. *Spiritual* creativity inspires us to venture into a divine realm and transcendental world. Creative beauty as a *spiritual foundation* produces connectedness to universal values and promotes healing and transformation.

Julia Cameron found that when people work on their spirituality, their creativity wakes up. And when people work on their creativity, their spirituality wakes up. She coaches people to make a solo date, once a week, to do something artful that interests or enchants them. "So, it might be going to a pet store. It might be going to a children's bookstore. It could be going to a gallery. It could be going to a botanical garden. The point is that it's fun." In a world filled with unsettledness, anxiety, and terror, the soul longs for its vision of divine beauty. For vision contributes to our desires in making meaning, reimagining worlds, and creating harmony and peace.

In his *Letter to Artists*, Pope St. John Paul II reaffirmed the important role of musicians, architects, writers, and painters, by saying, "May your art help to affirm that true beauty which, as a glimmer of the Spirit of God, will transfigure matter, opening the human soul to the sense of the eternal." Since one attribute of God is beauty, *beautiful* theophanies are always present to us. We need the "beautiful eyes of the soul" to see them.

The late Irish poet and luminous writer John O'Donohue claimed that once we awaken to the beauty that is God, there is a great sense of homecoming. In his book *Beauty*, he writes: "When we experience the Beautiful, there is a sense of homecoming. Some of our most wonderful memories are of beautiful places where we felt immediately at home. We feel most alive in the presence of the Beautiful for it meets the needs of our soul. For a while the strains of struggle and endurance are relieved, our frailty is illuminated by a different light in which we come to glimpse behind the shudder of appearances the sure form of things. In the experience of beauty, we awaken and surrender in the same act." When we, as creations of God, create or encounter the beautiful creations of others, something changes in us. We are moved. We are inspired.

The Holy Spirit uses beauty in art, poetry, and music to

capture our attention and engage our emotions. Our souls respond and challenge us to reflect on thought-provoking ideas, ways of being, or contrasting cultures. This artful influence subtlety evokes us to progress to a more noble and loving understanding of each other, ourselves, and God.

One Word at a Time

*There is always light. If only we are brave enough
to see it. If only we are brave enough to be it.*
—Amanda Gorman

Amanda Gorman's soul-stirring poetry is well known. "The Hill We Climb" touched our national hearts with hope and vision during the 2021 inaugural address and gained her international notoriety. Amanda started her dream early on as a youth delegate for the United Nations at sixteen and, that same year, founded One Pen One Page, a free creative-writing program for underserved youth. In 2017, she was the first Youth Poet Laureate in the United States. A Harvard graduate in 2020, she says we can expect to see her run for president in 2036.

In kindergarten, Amanda was diagnosed with an auditory disorder that gave her a speech impediment. An early voracious reader, hoarding dozens of books in her second-grade cubby, she said she "literally tried at one point to read two at a time, side by side." Obsessed, she wanted to learn everything, to read everything, to do everything, and was constantly on sensory overload. Her mom, an inner-city English elementary teacher, kept the TV off because she wanted her children to be engaged and active. So instead, they made forts, put on plays and musicals, and Amanda "wrote like crazy."

When she was in third grade, her teacher, Shelly Friedman, introduced her to poetry, and it was through writing and reciting poetry that she found her voice. Friedman recognized that Amanda's passion "could flower into something much bigger." In college, one way she worked to overcome her speech impediment was by singing a song loaded with *R*s from the

Pulitzer Prize–winning musical *Hamilton* by Lin-Manuel Miranda. The day after the 2021 inauguration, on *Good Morning America*, Miranda made a surprise appearance to congratulate her. "The right words in the right order can change the world, and you proved that yesterday," he told her. "Keep changing the world, one word at a time." Poetry is her way, and she invites everyone to contemplate his or her own ways and means for forces of change.

"Think about what you can do, you specifically, that others cannot," Amanda says. "I don't have millions of dollars to donate to the causes I cherish, or millions of followers to direct. But I can write a poem. I learned about the power of language to start social movements, energize revolutions, and bring about widespread change."

When asked what she hopes to accomplish with her voice, she responds, "I hope my writing can remind us of our best selves, even in testing times."

Creator, Creation, and Creativity

Many believe—and I believe—that I have been
designated for this work by God. In spite of my
old age, I do not want to give it up; I work out
of love for God, and I put all my hope in Him.
—Michelangelo

Our imaginations are shaped and transformed word by word, or stroke by stroke, by artists who masterfully create. Spiritual masterpieces are openings to God's creational, incarnational, and redeeming truths. One of the most famous interior painted spaces in the world is the Sistine Chapel. Michelangelo's faith and mysticism painted the frescoes of the Sistine Chapel depicting nine scenes from the Old Testament. It is truly a magnificent example of how an artist's creative genius can impact generations of souls through the beauty of art. In order to paint the high ceiling, Michelangelo devised his own wooden scaffolding and worked under difficult conditions standing upright for this work. He strained his head for four years, and so do the twenty-five thousand souls who go through the chapel daily to experience his awe-inspiring creation story.

James Romaine is an associate professor of art history at Lander University in Greenwood, South Carolina. He is also president and cofounder of the Association of Scholars of Christianity in the history of art. In his essay "Creator, Creation, and Creativity," featured in the book, *It Was Good: Making Art to the Glory of God,* Romaine emphasizes the value of the *true* artist who creates the "deeply mysterious and supernatural."

Romaine expresses his view that Michelangelo's iconic *The Creation of Adam* not only represents a moment of creation but employs the artist's own creativity as a means of studying God's creative nature. Rather than forming Adam out of dust, Michelangelo has God, through his outstretched finger, giving Adam *the spirit of creativity*. Therefore, for Romaine, before the fall, Adam was not "created to be a toiler but a *creative being*."

Looking at this new understanding, if our creative gifts are the image of God in us, then exploring and exercising them can be a means of relationship with God. This makes our works of art and our *artful living* a kind of visual and imaginative theology, inspiring us toward a more creative, dynamic, and living faith. This is grace, beauty, and, most importantly, love in action.

A Theology of Making

Our failure ... is that we fail to see the divine in
the earth, already active and working, pouring
forth grace and spilling glory into our lives.
Artists, whether they are professed believers or
not, tap into this grace and glory. There is a
'terrible beauty' operating throughout creation.
—Makoto Fujimura, *Silence and Beauty: Hidden*
Faith Born of Suffering

Like Michelangelo, some artists create art to capture a spiritual experience or revelation. It is both a spiritual process and a hope that their art may bring about a spiritual experience for others. One such master is Makoto Fujimura. A world-renowned fine artist, writer, and culture influencer, Makoto was born in Boston to Japanese parents but spent most of his childhood in Japan. Beauty is central to his idea of art. So is culture, but especially faith. In his book *Culture Care: Reconnecting with Beauty for Our Common Life,* Fujimura articulates that artists expose the soul's hunger for beauty and help to fill it, saying, "God asks us to continue as he began. We have the ability and responsibility to create more (gratuitous) beauty."

In his book *Art and Faith: A Theology of Making*, Fujimura proposes a "theology of making" or practicing one's spiritual beliefs through the creation of art. "I experience God, my Maker, in the studio. I am immersed in the art of creating, and I have come to understand this dimension of life as the most profound way of grasping human experience and the nature of our existence in the world. I call it the 'Theology of Making' ... It has become my point of reference for a lifetime of star-gazing into the infinite realities of beauty and the sacred—and then creating."

Fujimura believes that God is creator and that creating in the image of God is open to everyone, regardless of background or profession. Whether we are hair stylists, recycling collectors, UBER drivers, or CEOs, we are called by the great artist to cocreate. Fujimura promotes a vision of how *acts of creativity* relate to our faith. God created out of abundance and exuberance, and the universe (and we) exist because God *loves to create*. In this way, our cocreating acts confirm God's plan for the new creation to come. "God's design in Eden, even before the fall," he writes, "was to sing creation into being and invite God's creatures to sing with God, to cocreate into the creation."

In his book, suffering is also given particular focus in relation to new creation. Fujimura uses the Japanese art form of Kintsugi, in which broken pottery is re-formed using brilliant gold. Known as a metaphor for life, this artform embraces our brokenness, our hurts, and our failures. And with the healing force of grace, luminously, Kintsugi restructures a created work into something new, which, according to Fujimura, "Now becomes more beautiful and more valuable than the original, unbroken vessel. The gold highlights our scars and defines the beauty of resilience and potentiality for growth by the grace of God." Fujimura explains: "To me, the Holy Spirit is the true medium for any human expression. Our lives are the artworks of the Spirit, and our art can flow directly out of this relationship."

Robert Kushner wrote on Fujimura's art in *Art in America* this way: "The idea of forging a new kind of art, about hope, healing, redemption, refuge, while maintaining visual sophistication and intellectual integrity, is a growing movement, one which finds Makoto Fujimura's work at the vanguard."

Fujimura has sponsored the collaboration of art, culture, and faith by founding the International Arts Movement under which he established his Fujimura Institute. He also served as director of the Brehm Center for Worship, Theology, and the Arts at Fuller Theological Seminary 2015-2020.

He travels widely and recognizes the historic changes the world is experiencing and the role of art in empowering people to reflect, explore their feelings, and become more deeply aware. Expressing optimism, he reflects, "my work constitutes one of many voices calling for change, and I am increasingly hopeful as I observe evidence that we are all in a larger process of reexamining ourselves."

From Glory to Glory ...

Everything has beauty, but not everyone sees it.
—Confucius

Epiphaneia is the shining up and breaking forth of the radiance of *veiled* powerful grounds of being ... the beautiful and the glorious in this world as the revelation of God. Hans Urs von Balthasar, a Swiss Catholic priest and major theologian of the twentieth century, wrote, "Jesus Christ is the most beautiful form and splendor because as God, He is Beauty Itself." When we behold beauty in this world, we are actually seeing the glory of God, Jesus Christ, manifested as goodness and truth.

This is perfection. This is reality. This is supernatural. This is the mystical body, the cosmic Christ. William Blake expresses this concept well: "If the doors of perception were cleansed, everything would appear to man as it is, infinite." *Our human* life, metaphysically, leads to and flows from the one who is beauty. Bishop St. Irenaeus of Lyons, who has been called the father of Catholic theology, expands on this idea to say that the living human being *is* the glory (beauty) of God because we are God's *living* artwork.

Made in God's image, humanity is His most glorious work of art. According to Irenaeus, man and woman are *inherently* beautiful because as the created artwork of the Creator, we give glory to the Creator by radiating the beauty and glory *of* the Creator. This glory is our daily living in truth, beauty, and goodness. In this way, we are living "fully alive" as was God's first intention when He created us. As in the art form of Kintsugi, after Adam's fall, all humankind has been remade through Christ's redeeming love. We are a new creation, more beautiful than the former.

Our lives are intended to participate in divine communion rather than "shoulder an existence to be spurned and shed." We possess capacity to grow in communion with God and will *become* more like Him by desire. In other words, to be a "fully alive" human being means seeing God in everything and being seen by God in all that we do and are. It is a faith walk in the dreams God had when He created each one of us with love. Every moment of every day is given eternal significance as it has a place, a kairos, within God's plan, centered on the universe, the cosmic Christ, and the kingdom of love.

St. John experienced this. He saw and testified in his gospel, "We have come to know and to believe the love that God has for us. God is love, and whoever abides in love abides in God, and God abides in them" (1 John 4:16).

The Fathers of the Church called this participation in the divine life "divinization" (*theosis*). We are brought into the inner life of God, the loving communion between the Father, the Son, and the Holy Spirit. This spiritual union with God is glorious! It is the soul, fully active, as pure love—loving. It is a return to a *higher state* of Edenic consciousness. It is a daily walking and *being with God*, not only at the breezy time, four o'clock in the garden, but always. Eternally.

EPILOGUE

St. Thomas University in Houston was two blocks from Covenant House, and I attended daily Mass in the chapel every morning. If you would allow me, I would like to digress for a moment and just talk a little about the beauty of the sacred and the soul's growth in virtue and grace. I firmly believe that my spiritual life and vocation grew day by day through the graces and beauty of every Mass as I intimately *received* Jesus. He became a *living* part of me, and I became a *living* part of the Mystical Body of Christ though my daily *Amen* at communion, (which means *so be it*).

When one receives Holy Communion, one receives the body, blood, soul, and divinity of Jesus Christ. At the reception of the Eucharist, we are inundated with sanctifying grace and receive an increase in the virtues of faith, hope, and charity. We also receive sacramental grace that helps in times of temptation and in our daily work and living. All in all, our bodies receive the necessary graces to grow in holiness. As the grace continues, we are transformed, body and soul, "from glory to glory" (2 Corinthians 3:18), taking on the very image and likeness of the Lord. God's very life is poured into us.

It was at Mass at St. Thomas University's chapel that I found my first spiritual director who was a priest. He looked to me to be a living saint with his gentle, kind, and noble face, (very much like my present director). His homilies were simple and insightful. We met every two weeks for an hour. At the time, I was as considering two religious orders: the Missionaries of

Charity and the Carmelites. I was reading St. Elizabeth of the Trinity and Edith Stein, (St. Teresa Benedicta of the Cross).

St. Thérèse pictures and statues were appearing everywhere. It was almost annoying. She can be very persistent. However, I did not think I could be silent all day or be cloistered. Carmelite nuns live behind an enclosure. Most do not go out except for doctors' appointments, training classes, or certain funerals. It could be perceived as radical, and it is. You need grace to understand it and live it.

One year after St. Teresa of Calcutta's death anniversary, eight months into my Covenant House position, I wrote to the Missionaries of Charity to inquire about a come-and-see experience in Washington, DC.

Saint Teresa founded the Missionaries of Charity in Calcutta, about twenty-five years ago, and the order has grown into a worldwide network of 4,500 nuns operating nursing homes, orphanages, hospices, and other charitable programs. Because of my love for Covenant House, I was interested in working in an orphanage. Two weeks later, I received a letter stating I was too old to enter. The cutoff age was thirty-seven, and I was thirty-eight. I remember not feeling disappointment. I was still on an adventure, waiting for the next clue. So, at the time, I did nothing but wait.

Another two weeks went by, and I received another letter from the Missionaries of Charity. This one asked if I would be interested in coming to explore the contemplative branch of the order. When Mother Teresa started her order, she went to the Carmelites and asked them to pray for her and her work. St. Thérèse was the patron saint. However, as the years went by, St. Teresa started her own contemplative branch with the older Missionaries of Charity.

When I read that letter, I knew immediately that God was calling me to contemplative life. It was also apparent that if I was to be a contemplative, I would be a Carmelite. I was reading St. Teresa Benedicta's (Edith Stein's) book *The Hidden Life*, at the time of the second letter.

I looked up Carmelite Monasteries in Massachusetts, in a religious directory in our faith community office, and found one in Boston. Even though I grew up fifteen minutes from this Carmel, I never knew it was here. I called the same day and made an appointment to see the vocation director when I got home to Boston in February.

After a weekend come-and-see and a six-week summer live-in, I entered the following January on the Feast of the Baptism of Jesus. For the past twenty-three years, this grace-filled adventure has never ceased. Thank God, I am able to see my family frequently and my closest friends a few times a year. So, when people ask me what I miss most, I say, "The ocean."

But on certain days in the summer, if the breezes are just right, as I pass a screened door on the first floor, I will catch a few strong unmistakable whiffs of the sea.

Once, I was caught on my way to the choir for four o'clock Vespers. One of the sisters asked me what I was smelling with my head outstretched against the screen, breathing deeply.

"The ocean," I whispered.

But smiling to myself, I said, "My Dado."

CPSIA information can be obtained
at www.ICGtesting.com
Printed in the USA
BVHW040230260922
647977BV00004B/59